CW01647496

Seven Ways, Truths and Reasons Volume 2

White Tree Publishing

Seven Ways, Truths and Reasons Volume 2

Lin Wills
© Lin Wills 2024

This Paperback ISBN: 978-1-915671-25-7

Also available as an eBook
eBook ISBN: : 978-1-915671-24-0

All rights reserved. Without limiting the rights under copyright reserved above, no part of this publication may be reproduced, stored in a retrieval system, or transmitted, in any form or by any means (electronic, mechanical, photocopying, recording or otherwise), without the prior written permission of the copyright owner of this book.

Bible verses are from the Bible verses are taken from New American Standard Bible 1995 (NASB1995) New American Standard Bible®, Copyright © 1960, 1971, 1977, 1995 by The Lockman Foundation. All rights reserved.

Published by
White Tree Publishing
Bristol
UNITED KINGDOM
wtpbristol@gmail.com

For full list of books and updated information visit:
https://whitetreepublishing.com/

Contents

Introduction

When God led me to start the Seven Series, I never imagined there would be so many titles. We are currently eighty-six titles, all published as eBooks and many as booklets. A lot of people have been suggesting that I put them together in one book. So I put the first sixty-three in Volume 1, to make it easier for people who want to order printed copies. We now have Volume 2 with the next twenty-three short chapters!

As well as providing chapters of particular interest, this book can also be used as a devotional, as there are seven sections in each chapter, with Scripture references to look up in your own Bible each day.

I want to thank my very supportive husband Len. His encouragement and input, and ideas have been invaluable. I also want to thank Chris Wright of White Tree Publishing for all his support and help in so many ways. I am grateful for his God-centred input. I could not have done it without him.

I want to thank my daughter Lucy, and my son-in-law Matt for all their ongoing support and help right from the start. And thank you to my other daughter Victoria and son-in-law Laurence for their input. I also want to thank all those who constantly support us in input and in so many ways. Thank you, all, for your prayers, encouragement, gifts and love. Bless you all.

I live in England, and my husband Len and I are part of *Intercessors for Bristol*: Website:

http://www.intercessorsforbristol.org.uk/

We long to see God move in revival, and we have an itinerant ministry which covers a circuit of churches in our city and beyond on a regular basis.

We love to meet with God's people and encourage one another in His presence through worship, the Word of God, and the gifts of the Holy Spirit.

Our vision is to see God's people rise up in victory, and set on fire to be the powerful army God called us to be. We want to see all that the enemy has stolen from God's people restored back to the Church, and prayer and intercession released like never before.

Praying that this volume will be useful and a blessing to many people.

Lin Wills
Bristol UK

Website:
www.lenandlin.com

For more details
please contact Lin Wills:
hello@lenandlin.com

eBook editions of individual Chapters are published by White Tree Publishing, publishers of over 250 Christian books available from most eBook distributors.
https://whitetreepublishing.com/

All Scripture is inspired by God and profitable for teaching, for reproof, for correction, for training in righteousness; so that the man of God may be adequate, equipped for every good work
(2 Timothy 3:16-17).

1. Seven Truths about the Table

From this Chapter

A mother was dropping her son off at a Christian group. As she was leaving, she was asked, "Where are you going? There's a place set for you at the table. Are you not joining us?"

"Is there really a place set for me?"

The answer was, "Why yes, of course. We were expecting you."

It was just a passing comment, but God brought it back to me and started speaking to me about it – especially about the importance of it, because of how highly God values every one of us. All are welcome, a place is laid for all.

1. A place is laid

Our youngest daughter Lucy and our son-in-law Matt are living, working and serving the Lord in a church in Ephrata, Lancaster

County, USA. They completed Missional Discipleship training, and the Lord began to highlight others who wanted to do the same. So they began small huddles of five or six people in their home, providing food and going through the sessions each week.

When everyone was arriving, they had a mum drop off her son. They thought that both mother and son were attending, but when Matt saw her start to drive away, he ran after her and asked, "Where are you going? There's a place set for you at the table. Are you not joining us?"

She reversed back up the drive and went into the house and asked my daughter, "Is there really a place set for me?" The answer was, "Why yes, of course. We were expecting you."

It was just a passing comment, but God brought it back to me and started speaking to me about it – especially about the importance of it, because of how highly God values every one of us. All are welcome, for all a place is laid.

2. There is a place at the Table for all

2 Samuel 9:1-13: *Then David said, "Is there yet anyone left of the house of Saul, that I may show him kindness for Jonathan's sake?" ... Ziba said to the king, "There is still a son of Jonathan who is crippled in both feet.*

So the king said to him, "Where is he?"

Then King David sent and brought him from the house of Machir. ... And David said, "Mephibosheth."

And he said, "Here is your servant!"

David said to him, "Do not fear, for I will surely show kindness to you for the sake of your father Jonathan, and will restore to you all the land of your grandfather Saul; and you shall eat at my table regularly."

Again he prostrated himself and said, "What is your servant, that you should regard a dead dog like me?"

Then the king called Saul's servant Ziba and said to him, "All that belonged to Saul and to all his house I have given to your master's grandson. You and your sons and your servants shall cultivate the land for him, and you shall bring in the produce so that your master's grandson may have food; neverthe-

less Mephibosheth your master's grandson shall eat at my table regularly."

Now Ziba had fifteen sons and twenty servants. Then Ziba said to the king, "According to all that my lord the king commands his servant so your servant will do."

So Mephibosheth ate at David's table as one of the king's sons. ... So Mephibosheth lived in Jerusalem, for he ate at the king's table regularly.

This is the story of Mephibosheth, who was the only remaining member of Saul's house. He was Jonathan's son, and he was crippled in both feet. King David wanted to do an act of kindness to Mephibosheth because of his love for his father Jonathan.

David invited him to eat at his table in the Palace regularly. He gave Mephibosheth all that belonged to Saul and his house. He was Saul's grandson, so he ate at the King's table as one of the King's own sons. David had put all the servants at Mephibosheth's disposal!

What an act of kindness, way beyond the extra mile. What a massive change to Mephibosheth's life. He was adopted by the King, welcomed, loved and accepted. Because he could not walk, he was carried to the table. What a wealth, and abundance, a banquet for him – in the presence of the King.

This makes us realise what one act of kindness can do to change a person's life for ever. Kindness is powerful – it is a fruit of the Holy Spirit.

There is a place at the Table for all of us, whether we have taken our place yet or not. There is a place reserved for you. For each one of us. No one is left out of the Table of the Lord.

God never stops loving us – whatever we do, or don't do. His love is fixed, and unconditional. We are the objects of His love.

When Jesus died on the cross, it was God's way of saying to the whole world, "I love you."

John 15:13: Jesus said, *"Greater love has no one than this, that one lay down his life for his friends."*

If we say sorry for all the wrong things we have done, and mean it, and ask Jesus into our lives, He comes and changes us from within. We become a brand-new person on the inside. Old things pass away and all things become new. We are born again! We can now take our place at the Table. We belong, we are adopted as a child of God, and we have an inheritance that won't fade away.

John 14:1-6: Jesus said, *"Do not let your heart be troubled; believe in God, believe also in Me. In My Father's house are many dwelling places; if it were not so, I would have told you; for I go to prepare a place for you. If I go and prepare a place for you, I will come again and receive you to Myself, that where I am, there you may be also. And you know the way where I am going."*

Thomas said to Him, "Lord, we do not know where You are going, how do we know the way?"

Jesus said to him, "I am the way, and the truth, and the life; no one comes to the Father but through Me."

There is a place at the Table and a place in Heaven prepared for you. Jesus died to give you eternal life in Heaven with Him – for ever. He gives total forgiveness of all our sins, total love and acceptance as part of God's family – and a place at the Table with the King of kings!

3. It is a prepared Table

Psalm 23:5: *You prepare a table before me in the presence of my enemies; You have anointed my head with oil; My cup overflows.*

This Psalm is all about who our Shepherd is. This Shepherd has everything we need. There is no lack in Him. He is our protector and provider. We need to trust Him completely, because He is totally dependable. His goodness and mercy will be with us every day of our lives. Jesus knows each one of us by name, just as a shepherd knows his own sheep.

Our Shepherd knows us individually, and wants a close, intimate relationship with each one of us. The sheep follow their shepherd everywhere. He leads, and they rely on him. As we turn our cares over to our Shepherd, He fulfils His promise to us that we will lack nothing. In Him is everything we will ever need, and we prove this by depending on Him totally in every situation of our lives.

The prepared Table is a table that God prepares for us in "the presence of our enemies." The enemy cannot touch the prepared Table of the Lord.

The Lord's Table speaks of abundance, plenty, overflowing provision. It is a banquet in the presence of the King – all that we have inherited as children of the King. There is eternal life for us: love, joy, peace, freedom, identity, authority, power, victory, healing, restoration, blessing and favour.

Jesus left nothing out when He died on the cross. He covered it all, for all time and eternity. As He cried out, *"It is finished,"* (John 19:30) Jesus carried it all, so we wouldn't have to carry it.

We cannot eat at the Lord's Table and Satan's table too. Satan's table carries the things of the world that decay and fade away. Light and darkness don't mix. We make our own choice. We cannot sit on the fence.

2 Corinthians 3:2-3: *You are our letter, written in our hearts, known and read by all people, revealing yourselves, that you are a letter of Christ, delivered by us, written not with ink but with the Spirit of the living God, not on tablets of stone but on tablets of human hearts.*

When we make the right choice, then we become *living letters,* written on our hearts, not with pen and ink but with changed hearts for all to see and read. Jesus is the only way to Heaven. There is no other way!

4. Have you taken your place at the table?

Proverbs 3:3: *Do not let kindness and truth leave you; Bind them around your neck, Write them on the tablet of your heart.*

If we have taken our place at the Table, are we living in the good of it? Are we feasting on the abundance, or are we making do with snacks and leftovers? Where are we living? Are we living in what Jesus came to give us: Life in abundance?

The psalmist says in Psalm 23, *"My cup overflows."* Is *our* cup overflowing, or are we living on the dregs? Are we living close to Jesus, or far off? Are we drinking from the fountain that will never run dry? Are we feasting on His bountiful supply?

God is not a stingy God. Are we living in the land of "Not enough", in the land of "Just enough", or in the land of "More than enough"? God's supply never runs out!

If the Lord is our Shepherd, we shall not want. Are we saying something like this? "If only I had this or that, then everything would be great." Or, "If only that prayer could be answered in the way I wanted."

If only! It's good to trust God in all that He gives us, and still trust Him, that He knows best, and accept that the things He doesn't give us are for our own good.

We can miss out on what God wants to give us in the future, if we don't let go of the past. Any guilt or regrets of the past were all dealt with on the cross – so let it go, agree with God's Word, and live in the total provision and power and authority He has paid the price to give us.

1 John 1:9: *If we confess our sins, He is faithful and righteous to forgive us our sins and to cleanse us from all unrighteousness.*

Wherever we are today, God meets us there! Deuteronomy 8:7: *For the Lord your God is bringing you into a good land, a land of brooks of water, of fountains and springs, flowing forth in valleys and hills.*

5. Provision at the Table

2 Corinthians 9:8: *God is able to make all grace abound to you, so that always having all sufficiency in everything, you may have an abundance for every good deed*

Romans 15:13: *Now may the God of hope fill you with all joy and peace in believing, so that you will abound in hope by the power of the Holy Spirit*

1 Peter 1:8: *And though you have not seen Him, you love Him, and though you do not see Him now, but believe in Him, you greatly rejoice with joy inexpressible and full of glory.*

Philippians 4:7 and 19: *And the peace of God, which surpasses all comprehension, will guard your hearts and your minds in Christ Jesus. ... And my God will supply all your needs according to His riches in glory in Christ Jesus.*

Psalm 104:15: *And wine which makes man's heart glad, so that he may make his face glisten with oil, and food which sustains man's heart.*

Are we enjoying the lush green pastures? Or is the land barren? We need fresh oil poured over us every day. We need to magnify the King, not our problems. No opposition can stop God's purposes.

We will set the enemy to flight with the weapons God gives us – the weapons of prayer, worship, fellowship, the Word of God which is the sword of the Spirit. We need to use our weapons *daily*. We will break through the clouds and the storm as we focus on the King. We will touch the triumphant victory of God in our situation.

Corrie ten Boom said, *"If you look at the world, you'll be distressed. If you look within, you'll be depressed. If you look at God you'll be at rest. ... If you want to be defeated, look back. If you want to be distracted, look around. But if you want to be delivered, look up."* We need to keep our focus on the King.

5. Knowing our *own* place at the Table

Knowing my place – taking my place.
Living in the provision – of my place.
Moving in the vision – of my place.
Living in the truth of it being a prepared place – in the presence of my enemies.
Keeping my focus – in my place.
Living in the richness and abundance – of my place.
Knowing the favour and total acceptance and love of my Father – in my place.
Living in the power of my identity and uniqueness – in my place.
Being totally abandoned and submitted to Him – in my place.
Praying and interceding for others who have not taken their place – in my place.
Reaching out to others with God's love and compassion to a hurt and dying world – in *my* place, so that others can take *their* place!

7. Ten points to finish

1. There *is* a place at the Table for you.
2. You *are* highly valued by God.
3. The Table is prepared in the presence of your enemies.
4. But the enemy cannot touch it.
5. The Lord *is* my Shepherd – I shall not want.
6. Jesus said, *"I go to prepare a place for you."*
7. Live in the abundance of life.
8. Leave the past behind.
9. Wherever we are, God meets us *there*!
10. Live in the land of Plenty.

A prayer, if you would like to use it

Dear Lord, pleases help me to live in the abundant life that You died to give me, that I will feast at Your Table and drink from Your Fountain of Life, living in Your refreshment and power every day.

Fill me afresh with Your Holy Spirit. Anoint me with fresh oil.

In Jesus' Name. Amen.

A prayer if you would like to ask Jesus into your life

Dear Lord Jesus, I am tired of sitting on the fence. I want to thank You for dying on the cross for me, so I can be with You in Heaven when I leave this earth.

I am sorry for all the things I have done wrong in my life. Please forgive me. I ask You to come into my life and change my heart. Make me a brand-new person on the inside, and fill me with Your Holy Spirit.

In Jesus' Name. Amen.

If you prayed this prayer, and meant it, you are now born again. Don't keep it to yourself – tell someone. And find a good church to belong to that preaches and worships Jesus, and reaches out to others that need to know Him too.

2. Seven Ways to Leave the Past Behind

From this Chapter

God is always wanting to move us on – season to season, blessing to blessing. Last season will not fit into this season. We need to guard against stagnating. We need to leave behind what belongs to the past.

Every season is different, and what is a blessing in one season can become a blockage in another season – if it is something we should have finished with. God doesn't shrink us – He wants to stretch us!

Let us be willing to move on to where God wants to take us *now*, letting go of everything that could hold us back. We must not allow the enemy to rob us. What we refuse to get over, we will live under.

1. Never build walls around past blessings

Matthew 17:1-5: *Six days later Jesus took with Him Peter and James and John his brother, and led them up on a high mountain by themselves. And He was transfigured before them; and His face shone like the sun, and His garments became as white as light.*

And behold, Moses and Elijah appeared to them, talking with Him. Peter said to Jesus, "Lord, it is good for us to be here; if You wish, I will make three tabernacles here, one for You, and one for Moses, and one for Elijah."

While he was still speaking, a bright cloud overshadowed them, and behold, a voice out of the cloud said, "This is My beloved Son, with whom I am well-pleased; listen to Him!"

Peter wanted to capture the moment and keep it – by staying and putting up tents! But however wonderful the blessing, we must not make it a shrine. Move on with God, because there is always much more. We must guard against putting yesterday's blessings in the place of what God wants to give us *now*!

God is always wanting to move us on – season to season, blessing to blessing. Last season will not fit into this season. We need to guard against stagnating. We need to leave behind what belongs to the past.

Every season is different, and what is a blessing in one season can become a blockage in another season – if it is something we should have finished with.

In verse 5 of Matthew 17 we notice that while Peter is still speaking, a cloud overshadows them and God's voice says, *"This is My beloved Son, with whom I am well-pleased; listen to Him!"*

And in verse 8 it says that as they lifted up their eyes, *they saw no one except Jesus Himself alone*. Our main focus has to be on Jesus, not on man.

Psalm 118:8-9: *It is better to take refuge in the Lord than to trust in man. It is better to take refuge in the Lord than to trust in princes.*

2. Be willing for the new thing God wants to do

Isaiah 43:18-19: *"Do not call to mind the former things, Or ponder things of the past. "Behold, I will do something new, Now it will spring forth; Will you not be aware of it? I will even make a roadway in the wilderness, Rivers in the desert.*

Our future is not tied to anything we have lost in the past, unless we allow it. We need to rise up and take back any ground the enemy has stolen, then press forward into our future with God.

We need to finish with what God wants us to finish with, so that what is ahead can be unlocked. God brings the beginning out of the end.

It's good to speak to the mountains of the past, and to see old cycles broken in our lives. Then we can receive the blessing of the *here* and the *now*!

We must never resist the new thing that God wants to do in our lives – to perceive it. As the dictionary defines it, "Understand through the senses."

We need to hear what the Holy Spirit is saying to us, and then obey Him. Coming into alignment with God daily, day by day, moment by moment, we are Kingdom people in the Earth, bringing glory to His Name.

"Your kingdom come. Your will be done, On earth as it is in heaven" Matthew 10:11

3. **We need to get rid of any clutter**

Philippians 3:13: *Brethren, I do not regard myself as having laid hold of it yet; but one thing I do: forgetting what lies behind and reaching forward to what lies ahead.*

Clutter can seem heavy on us and oppressive, especially from the past. Things like past mistakes, regrets, resentment and so on. Some people call it baggage. These things will keep us stuck in the past if we allow them to.

Paul had lots of clutter in his past. He played a part in destroying churches and putting God's people in prison. Paul had to choose to forget the past, otherwise he would not have been able to fulfil what God had called him to do. He said, *"One thing I do: forgetting what lies behind and reaching forward to what lies ahead*" Philippians 3:13. When Paul decided to forget the past, God gave him what he needed to go forward and move on.

If we dwell on the past it will grip us. We need to stop thinking about it, or the enemy will constantly put the past in front of us, causing us to become stuck in it. And then we can't move forward.

We are not victims of our thoughts. We can choose what we think about. Philippians 4:8: *Finally, brethren, whatever is true, whatever is honorable, whatever is right, whatever is pure, whatever is lovely, whatever is of good repute, if there is any excellence and if anything worthy of praise, dwell on these things.*

The power of the truth of God's Word will renew our minds. If we are carrying guilt about our past, we need to receive God's forgiveness – and forgive ourselves. Then God will free us and help us to move into the future He has planned for us. He knows our hearts and our intentions. If we decide to let the past go, and are willing to do whatever God tells us to do, He will run to help us and free as from the grip of the past.

4. We need to step up to another level

Ephesians 3:20-21: *Now to Him who is able to do far more abundantly beyond all that we ask or think, according to the power that works within us, to Him be the glory in the church and in Christ Jesus to all generations forever and ever. Amen.*

God always wants to elevate us and enlarge us, and take us deeper with Him. He doesn't want us to build walls around anything. Blessings of the past, the pain of the past, relationships of the past – *anything* of the past.

There is a difference between us encouraging ourselves about what *God* has done in the past, than the past being something that plays on our minds in a negative way, holding us back from the fullness of what God has for us now.

Dwelling on the past can also cause us to have a mindset that tells us it was "better in those days." We need to look back and learn. Negative reflection can become positive reflection, rather than being stuck in the past. If we don't learn, then there is every possibility we will repeat the mistakes and faults of the past in the future.

Ecclesiastes 7:10: *Do not say, "Why is it that the former days were better than these?" For it is not from wisdom that you ask about this.*

We can get more excited about the past than the future as we get older. But look at Caleb. When he was 85 years old he said, *"I am still as strong today as I was in the day Moses sent me; as my strength was then, so my strength is now, for war and for going out and coming in. Now then, give me this hill country about which the Lord spoke on that day, for you heard on that day that Anakim were there, with great fortified cities; perhaps the Lord will be with me, and I will drive them out as the Lord has spoken"*(Joshua 14:11-12). Give me the mountain!

He was living in the power of the present, believing in a Mighty God! We must never stop reaching and stretching, no matter what age we are. Let's go forward with God into the future He has planned for us.

5. Live in the Power of the Present

1 Kings 19:21: *So he* [Elisha] *returned from following him* [Elijah], *and took the pair of oxen and sacrificed them and boiled their flesh with the implements of the oxen, and gave it to the people and they ate. Then he arose and followed Elijah and ministered to him.*

How can we make the most of the power of the present right now? Hearing God today, coming into alignment with Him today, doing His will, loving him with all our hearts. We need to be that "living sacrifice."

In 1 Kings 19:21 we read about Elisha going as Elijah's assistant. Earlier in chapter 19 we see that Elijah hears God speak to him, not in the earthquake, wind or fire, but in the gentle whisper. God instructs him to go and anoint Elisha, so Elijah finds Elisha and throws his coat over his shoulders as a sign that he has now been chosen.

Are we walking closely enough to God to hear the gentle

whisper? What a difference it would have made in Elisha's life if Elijah hadn't heard and obeyed. But he did hear, and as a result Elisha returned to his oxen and killed them, and used the wood from the plough to build a fire to cook them. He gave the meat to the people. They had a feast, and then Elisha went with Elijah as his assistant.

Elisha obeyed and finished with everything to take up God's call. He burnt his bridges and his living! He had no Plan B. No "just in case." He heard God's call and went. He left behind everything that would hold him back.

He stepped into the newness and freshness of what God was doing with him – *now*!

6. **Learn to flow with what God is doing**

Galatians 5:16: *But I say, walk by the Spirit, and you will not carry out the desire of the flesh.*

We need to learn to flow with the Holy Spirit, not dragging back to the shore, the safe place. We need to get our feet wet, move out into the depths with God. The treasure is in the deep places.

We are living in a time of many challenges and changes. God is sifting us and stirring us up, preparing us for what He is doing in these days. God is never doing nothing.

It's good to ask God what *our* part is in what He is doing. God wants us to enter in with all of our heart, and yield to the Holy Spirit. Let's raise the level of our expectancy in our Great and Mighty God!

There are greater heights to reach, greater blessings to come, greater depths to swim in. Let's make up our minds to press on and win the victory over the giants in the land. The enemy is already defeated. *But in all these things we overwhelmingly conquer through Him who loved us* (Romans 8:37).

7. **Live in the good of today's Manna**

Exodus 16:19-20: *Moses said to them, "Let no man leave any of it until morning." But they did not listen to Moses, and some left part of it until morning, and it bred worms and became foul;*

and Moses was angry with them.

There was just enough Manna for each day. Fresh every day. It was God's provision. But when the people disobeyed Moses and kept it overnight, it went stale and stank, and was riddled with worms!

God gives us exactly what we need for each day, which is more than enough. We need to make the most of who He is to us *today*. Each morning His benefits are new. Lamentations 3:22-23: *The Lord's lovingkindnesses indeed never cease, for His compassions never fail. They are new every morning; great is Your faithfulness.*

What does stepping up with God look like? Being fully on fire for Him? How much of our day and our service for Him is totally because of His power at work within us? Maybe we need to press into God for more of His power, and hunger for more of His Presence in our lives.

What kind of God would want to leave us where we are, where we are comfortable, not reaching and stretching for more in case we get hurt, only doing what we are capable of and comfortable with?

God doesn't shrink us – He wants to stretch us!

Let us be willing to move on to where God wants to take us *now*, letting go of everything that could hold us back. We must not allow the enemy to rob us. What we refuse to get over, we will live under.

Anything we don't forgive, we will drag like a ball and chain. Take hold of what God is giving us *now*! The time we have is *now*! How can we embrace the power of the present more than we are doing – right now?

A prayer if you would like to use it

Dear Lord Jesus, help me to leave the past behind, to get rid of any clutter, to forgive and receive Your forgiveness. Help me to forgive myself. Help me not to build walls around anything of the past, but to move on with You, and fully embrace the power of the present.

In Jesus' Name. Amen.

3. Seven Truths about Rejection

From this Chapter

If we know we have God's full acceptance, then we are not fearful of rejection. God has given each of us our calling and our destiny that no one else can fulfil. We need to accept our value and worth in God, and reject rejection and the lies of the enemy about our lack of worth. No matter how it came to us, feelings of rejection originate from the enemy, because he is the Father of lies. We need to exchange the lies for the truth of God's Word.

1. Rejection is one of Satan's most powerful weapons
John 10:10: *The thief comes only to steal and kill and destroy; I came that they may have life, and have it abundantly.*

The enemy uses rejection very often to keep people from coming to faith in God. He also uses it to stunt our spiritual growth. Rejection can have a really negative effect on our relationships.

Rejection gives us a distorted understanding of God and His character as a loving Heavenly Father who wants only the best for us. Rejection takes away our confidence in ourselves and in what God has placed within us. It can make us feel worthless, and undeserving, and less valuable than others.

Jesus was rejected. He was betrayed. Rejection hurts. We need to bring rejection to Jesus' feet. There are so many emotions tied up in rejection.

Doubting God's goodness is one emotion. Being angry that we allowed ourselves to be hurt is another. So is being discouraged. God understands our hurt. He knows what it is like. Jesus experienced everything that we go through. He knew the feeling and pain of His separation from His Father on the cross.

Rejection can leave us feeling angry with God. Whatever we feel, we need to face up to it – then take it to Jesus. We need to work through it with Him, and let Him teach us through it. Let rejection be a gain, not a loss experience in our lives.

2. We need to admit how we feel

Hebrews 4:15: *For we do not have a high priest who cannot sympathize with our weaknesses, but One who has been tempted in all things as we are, yet without sin.*

Jesus is touched with our feelings. He knows – He has been there! And if we feel the need, it's good to talk to a wise and trusted friend, or a counsellor. It's good to be around those who really love us and care for us in the right way.

We must not allow the enemy to play on our feelings of rejection. He can use them to get us into the wrong company. As we make the right choices, God helps us to do be in the right company. He gives us what we need.

Stand on the truth of God's Word. Keep open to the Holy Spirit to bring healing and restoration. Feelings of rejection are only for a time. They won't last for ever. God is still a good God and He will never let us down. Don't take rejection of the gospel personally. If people can't receive the truth, it's because their eyes have not been opened yet by the Holy Spirit. In this situation it's usually a rejection of what we believe, not of who we are.

Some people will be our enemies, but we are told to pray for them, and keep our hearts right and not get bitter (Matthew 5:44). Jesus will draw people to Him by His Spirit. We plant and we water, but God gives the increase. We need to look at how we do things, at our attitude to others. Are we too strong or forceful? (Colossians 3:17).

Is it more important to make our point, or to share the truth of Jesus in love? (2 Timothy 2:24). We need patience and grace with others. Testimony is great. It's our own experience, and it's powerful. No one can take that away. We need to empathise with others, and be sensitive to their feelings.

3. We are adopted!

Romans 8:15: *For you have not received a spirit of slavery leading to fear again, but you have received a spirit of adoption as sons by which we cry out, "Abba! Father!"*

We know if we are really loved for who we are. As we love with God's love, people will notice, they will see the difference. Sharing Jesus starts with relationship and sharing His love. God's timing is perfect as He works in our lives.

We need to align ourselves with that, and walk in obedience to the Holy Spirit. It's not about us – it's about Jesus! If we have known rejection at any time in our lives, we can end up agreeing with others' opinions of us, and always feel inferior and inadequate, or second-best.

However, we must be careful not to see loving criticism and advice as rejection. God speaks to us through others! Proverbs 19:20: *Listen to counsel and accept discipline, that you may be wise the rest of your days.* And if you are giving give advice to others, do it: *with all humility and gentleness, with patience, showing tolerance for one another in love* (Ephesians 4:1-2).

Rejection is not the truth about our worth. People's value of us, if they reject us, is usually wrong. It is only God's value of us that is right. We can't change people – God has to do that. God totally accepts us. We are blessed, chosen, loved, accepted, and adopted into God's family.

In order to know what our value is, we need to understand how God sees us. Don't let people who reject us put a value on us. God develops us through pain and hardships. He uses it for our own good. Jesus knew a lot of rejection. He was betrayed, denied, abandoned. He knew loneliness and suffering and rejection (Isaiah 53:4-5). In God's family we are totally loved and accepted.

4. Focus on God

Isaiah 26:3: *"The steadfast of mind You will keep in perfect peace, Because he trusts in You.*

We need to praise and thank Him for who He is, and for the blessings He showers on us. It is a choice we make. If we stay focused on God and His goodness and value of us, rejection will not be a hindrance or blockage to our spiritual growth. Knowing the truth sets us free.

It is the truth of the Word of God that we need to live by, not by what others say or what the enemy's lies tell us. We must leave everything alone that does not line up with God's truth. We need to reject any thoughts, words, or actions that don't line up with God's Word. God made us in His image (Psalm 139:4). We need to accept the truth that we are beautiful in God's eyes. The Holy Spirit convinces us of our beauty through Jesus.

We were made for a purpose, and God has a plan and purpose for each of us. We were made by Him and for Him. God loves us individually and intimately. He can heal all our hurt and pain – past, present, and future. And through it we can help others. He knows our hearts (Psalm 147:3). We are Kingdom people, accepted in the family of God!

5. Overcoming rejection!

1 John 3:1: *See how great a love the Father has bestowed on us, that we would be called children of God; and such we are. For this reason the world does not know us, because it did not know Him.*

Rejection can make us inclined to want to keep everyone happy! That will never work. It's an unreal expectation. Rejection can convince us that we have to put up with certain things because we feel it's what we deserve, otherwise we may get rejected again! It can make us believe that we don't need others. It's not true, but we try to convince ourselves that it is. So loneliness sets in. We can get defensive with others to make sure we don't get hurt again, and that just isolates us.

If we are seeing ourselves with a low self-worth, others will pick that up and treat us accordingly. Our self-worth is to be based only on God's opinion of us, otherwise we are too vulnerable to the opinion of others. When that happens, we allow their opinion of us to carry too much weight, and we find criticism very hard to take.

God wants us to know and understand how unique and amazing He has made us to be. *This* is how we get victory over rejection!

6. You are precious and honoured

Isaiah 43:4: *"Since you are precious in My sight, Since you are honored and I love you, I will give other men in your place and other peoples in exchange for your life.*

Repeated rejection can make us fearful that we are inadequate. In valuing ourselves, we show others how to value us.

If we know we have God's full acceptance, then we are not fearful of rejection. God has given each of us are calling and the destiny that no one else can fulfil.

We need to accept our value and worth in God, and refuse rejection and the lies of the enemy about our lack of worth. No matter how it came to us, feelings of rejection originate from the enemy, because he is the Father of lies. We need to exchange the lies for the truth of God's Word.

God disciplines us because He loves us too much to leave us where we are. He wants us to reach our highest potential – so don't let anyone put this down. We mustn't be afraid to be our unique selves when we are with others. Our confidence needs to come from within us, not from our evaluation of those around us. Again let me say, rejection is *not* the same as loving criticism and advice!

7. Be secure. Know who we are and what we are called to do

2 Timothy 1:7: *For God has not given us a spirit of timidity, but of power and love and discipline.*

We must know that God has called us, equipped us, and given us everything we need in order to reach our full potential in Him. We need to know who we are in God. We are totally loved and secure in Him. He rejoices over us with singing. We are the apple of His eye.

We are never a disappointment to Him. He believes in us, and in what He has placed within us, and He can see the finished picture of what we will be!

We need to agree with Him, and believe in ourselves. We are children of the Kingdom. We need to keep these things in our hearts and minds when others reject us, and pull away from us. If we focus on the truth of who we are in God, we are not at the mercy of what others think of us.

If we feel insecure, then fear can cause us to become man-pleasers. Our security must be in God alone, and in pleasing Him. We need to be ready to cover new ground with God – even if it means taking risks. If we are not willing to risk change, then we won't grow. We are wonderfully made and called by God! (Psalm 139).

A Prayer

Dear Lord,

Please help me with any rejection in my life. Help me to know who I am in You, and all that You have placed within me as Your child.

Help me to be secure in Your love. Teach me to know and live by Your truth, so that any lies will be dispelled from my mind and my life. Heal and restore me now, Lord.

In Jesus' Name. Amen.

4. Seven Truths about Restoration

From this Chapter

Restoration is not always to receive *more* than has been lost, but God's restoration is *beyond measure!* As we spend time with God in His presence, we are being transformed as we gaze upon Him. He is preparing us, positioning us, empowering us and restoring us. In His presence we can let it all go without losing anything, but gaining everything. Things take place here that don't take place anywhere else. We need to come here often, and give God quality time.

1. God's restoration plan for mankind
Romans 3:23: *For all have sinned and fall short of the glory of God*

Restoration is not always to receive *more* than has been lost, but God's restoration is *beyond measure!* Job is a great example of this (Job 42:10). God is a restoring God. He never wants to leave us where we are. Anything that has been stolen from us by the enemy, God wants to restore to us with added extra! Restoration is God's plan. It is His heart, and it includes all of us. He is doing a restoring work in our lives even now.

God's desire and purpose is to restore us fully to what He planned for us originally. God's original plan was for us to live in His Presence and His glory. Salvation's plan restores us to God through Jesus' death on the cross.

If we are not with Christ, God wants to see us restored in fellowship with Him through the blood of Jesus. Through Him, we come to God and are totally forgiven – of everything we have ever done wrong in our lives.

God saves us and restores us into His presence as we confess our sin, and invite Jesus to come into our lives. Jesus is the only way to heaven. There is no other way. We are saved by Him from eternal death to eternal life – from the darkness into the light. We are transformed by God's power and Spirit at work in our lives. We become a brand-new person inside!

2. God's restoration plan for His Church

Isaiah 43:18-19: *"Do not call to mind the former things, Or ponder things of the past. "Behold, I will do something new, Now it will spring forth; Will you not be aware of it? I will even make a roadway in the wilderness, Rivers in the desert."*

God is doing a new thing. He is restoring to the Church all that the enemy has stolen. He is restoring holiness and purity. He is restoring intimacy in His presence, passionate worship and the supernatural power of His Holy Spirit. There are signs, wonders, and miracles. Passion, vision, faith, prayer and intercession.

God is raising up His army in the land to stand strong against the enemy and his plans. He is preparing us for the fulfilment of His purposes on the Earth in these last days. He is raising us up to do things that will bring glory to God.

Ground that the enemy has stolen is being restored to the Church (Joel 2:28). God is speaking about the end times and pouring out His Spirit on us – both young and old Christians who will really take hold of God. His purposes will be fulfilled. His plan for His Church will come to pass, and bring Him glory!

God is restoring us to know and live in the abundant life, knowing our position in Christ, seated with Him in heavenly places to demonstrate His power and glory in the earth.

God is always working in us, changing us from glory to glory. He is shaping us, sifting us and stirring us. There are many challenges and changes ahead, and yet great blessing is happening at the same time. God is moving in our land. We need to be willing to come into alignment with Him, to be ready to come into the freshness of what He is doing in these days.

We can do what God says we can do. We are more than conquerors in His strength! (Acts 2:42-47).

Herschel B Dean says, "The average church is without New Testament excitement because we have regarded ourselves of engineers of a program rather than instruments that can demonstrate His Power."

3. Renewed strength

Isaiah 40:31: *Yet those who wait for the Lord Will gain new strength; They will mount up with wings like eagles, They will run and not get tired, They will walk and not become weary.*

Restoration is God's plan for everyone, to restore everyone to His original design and intentions for their life. This Scripture in Isaiah tells us about waiting on God and renewing our strength. Rising up comes from waiting on Him. "Abiding in the vine is more productive than activity!" Herschel B Dean.

There is so much happening to us. As we spend time with God in His presence, we are being transformed as we gaze upon Him. He is preparing us, positioning us, empowering us and restoring us. In His presence we can let it all go without losing anything but gaining everything. Things take place here that don't take place anywhere else. We need to come here often, and give God quality time.

Jesus again is our example as He left the crowd to be with His Father (Mark 1:35). Jesus knew His source. Busyness is not always the sign of fruitfulness. What an example we have in Jesus! Our close connection to Jesus, the vine, is how we bring forth much fruit. Abiding is staying, dwelling, living, not just coming and going, but spending quality time with Jesus.

It is the time to wait, to listen, to be at home. It's the time to have a good root system going down into the River of Life. Not rushed or hurried, but focused and uninterrupted. It is the time when strength is being renewed and restored.

4. God forgives and restores!

Luke 15:18: *I will get up and go to my father, and will say to him, "Father, I have sinned against heaven, and in your sight."*

The story of the prodigal son in Luke 15:11-24 tells us that there are two sons, and the younger son wants his inheritance early. So the father divides his wealth between his two sons. The younger son goes out and wastes his money on wild living and prostitutes. Then a famine hits the land, and he begins to starve. He ends up in a pigsty! So he decides to go home to his father and say sorry for his sin, and maybe his father will give him a job. He feels unworthy to be called his father's son after what he has done.

But as the father sees him coming – the long way off – he runs to embrace him and kisses him and welcomes him home. In that culture fathers never ran, but this father did!

Even if we fail God badly, there is always a way home. We have a loving, gracious heavenly Father who forgives us and welcome us with open arms as we cry out to Him in repentance, and turn away from our sin. He not only forgives us, but totally restores us into the family of God, into our rightful place. Everything totally restored to us (1 John 1:9).

When God's Word tells us He has forgiven us, we must receive it and accept it. The enemy will make us feel unworthy of it, but of course we never will be *worthy* of God's forgiveness. God's forgiveness is not based on us being worthy of it, it is based on what Jesus has already done for us on the cross. His sacrifice covers every sin. He, who was perfect and spotless, became sin for us. He carried it for us so we won't have to carry it. In *Him* we are made worthy. And it is all by His grace. Grace means undeserved favour (Ephesians 2:8-9). So when God forgives us, we need to agree with Him and forgive ourselves!

5. Put the past behind us

Joel 2:25: The Lord says, *"Then I will make up to you for the years That the swarming locust has eaten, The creeping locust, the stripping locust and the gnawing locust, My great army which I sent among you."*

God will restore to us the years and the ground has been lost. And more besides! We need to leave the past behind so we can go forward into the future. Whatever we have known in the past, God can use for good in our future.

Sometimes things happen beyond our control, but we know that the God who is in control will turn it for good in our lives. God takes ugly situations and turns them into something beautiful for His glory.

Our past doesn't determine our future, nor do other people or circumstances. It is God alone who does that (Jeremiah 29:11). God's plan for us will rule over every other plan – if we really want it to.

Whatever mistakes we have made in the past, as we ask God for forgiveness He will forgive us, so we can then move on. Before Paul's conversion, he was involved with persecuting Christians and shutting down churches. This was his *past*. Paul was *forgetting what lies behind and reaching forward to what lies ahead* (Philippians 3:13).

Dwelling on past sin and wallowing in guilt, just emphasises our failure. We need to receive our forgiveness and move on with God. We must let go of yesterday in order to live in today's blessing, and not allow our past to destroy our future. Letting go sets us free to go forward with God, into the future He has for us – in total restoration! No matter how broken we are, if we turn to God He will restore us to Himself (Isaiah 42:3).

He will not crush the weakest reed. What a gentleness and

grace comes through these words from Isaiah. God bends down to heal and restore us. He makes us whole. It is never too late to ask God to restore us. But why wait?

6. Burn our bridges

1 Kings 19:21: *So he* [Elisha] *returned from following him* [Elijah], *and took the pair of oxen and sacrificed them and boiled their flesh with the implements of the oxen, and gave it to the people and they ate. Then he arose and followed Elijah and ministered to him.*

Elisha's ministry began with burning everything that was his living! He couldn't go back to his old way of living, because he had destroyed it. He went to follow Elijah from that moment on. It was the end of his farming as he went to be Elijah's assistant. It was the start of a new season. The first step into something new is always the hardest.

The first step is not just taking a step into the future, it is dealing with and removing the possibility of going into the past. This is what Elisha did. He removed Plan B! It was plan A or nothing. To begin a new season we have to end the old season. Removing Plan B was an act of faith. No turning back, whatever happened!

If all we want is God's way, we will not entertain a Plan B. It is a radical relying on God – or nothing! Only *His* plan will do. Are we willing to burn our bridges, to prove God's provision, His guidance, and His restoration plan in our lives? Are we willing to be fully alive in God's Plan and purpose in our lives? To be fully alive in God Plan and purpose for us is to be fully present in the here and now. God is "The Great I AM" not, "the Great I was."

It's not good to hang on too tightly to what God did for us last time, however good it was (see Luke 9:32-33). On the Mount of Transfiguration Peter wanted to stay and put up three shelters. And then came God's voice, "This is My Beloved Son. Listen to Him."

If we build walls around past blessings we are in danger of missing what God wants to do next. It is good to be reminded of the greatness and faithfulness of God in the past, to encourage our faith in the future. But God is always at work in our lives with greater things to come. He is always doing something. He is the ever-present God, and we can prove Him, right here and right now!

7. Let God restore our love for Him

Deuteronomy 6:5: *You shall love the Lord your God with all your heart and with all your soul and with all your might.*

God wants all of our "Heart." He wants us to seek Him, to love Him, and trust Him (Proverbs 3:5 and Jeremiah 29:13).

We have to ask ourselves, do we love Him with all our heart? Do we trust Him with all of our heart? Do we seek Him with all of our heart? Are we standing strong in our faith when it means pain or pressure?

Prayer and the Word of God hold us strong and steady, when otherwise we may want to give up and move outside God's will for us.

If we have been hurt, this can sometimes hold us from stepping out in faith and taking risks again, in case we get hurt again. If we hold back, we can become unfruitful.

We are believing a lie if we think that there is a safer, better way than being in the will of God. The safest place on earth is being in the centre of God's will for us.

God showed me in a dream that being with Him, walking on water is as safe or even safer than walking on solid ground. The key is that we are with Him, walking with Him, listening to Him, praying to Him, loving Him with all our heart – and putting His Kingdom before anything else. This is the most powerful, safest place of all.

We must not allow the disappointments and setbacks of life to make our love for Him grow cold. It is too high a price to pay. We lose too much. We need to allow God to restore our love, our passion, our desire, our hunger for Him and His presence again if we feel we have grown cold. Then we will see that which is dead brought to life again for the glory of His Name, and the extension of His Kingdom.

A prayer

Thank you, Lord, that You are a restoring God. Please help me to know Your restoration fully in my life in every area. Help me to leave the past behind and step forward into the future with You. And help me to love You with all of my heart.

In Jesus' Name. Amen

A prayer if you want to ask Jesus into your life for the first time

Dear Lord Jesus,

I'm sorry for the things I have done wrong in my life. Please forgive me. Thank You for dying for me on the cross to set me free from my sin.

Please come into my life and fill me with Your Holy Spirit, and be with me for ever.

In Jesus' Name. Amen.

5. Seven Truths about Disappointment

From this Chapter

What is God's promise in our disappointment? We must never give in or give up with God. There is always a way forward. There are times when we need to pour out our feelings to someone we trust, otherwise we can end up in despair. But we need to make sure that we run to God first, with our heartaches and disappointments. God's ears are always open to our cries. We need to pour out our hearts to Him. He understands us and our discouragement – and our feelings of heartache. He has been there!

1. There is always a way forward with God
Psalm 42:11: *Why are you in despair, O my soul? And why have you become disturbed within me? Hope in God, for I shall yet praise Him, The help of my countenance and my God.*

When things don't go the way we think they should, we can

get disappointed. We all know feelings of disappointment. Following Jesus does not keep us from trouble and setbacks.

When our dreams have been shattered, life does not end there. God's purpose for us is still intact. Our disappointments can turn into God-appointments for us. He is still in charge and on the throne. There will still be His purpose for us to fulfil, and He will still give us all that we need to fulfil it.

We must never give in or give up with God. There is always a way forward. There are times when we need to pour out our feelings to someone we trust, otherwise we can end up in despair. But we need to make sure that we run to God first, with our heartaches and disappointments. God's ears are always open to our cries. We need to pour out our hearts to Him. He understands us and our discouragement – and our feelings of heartache. He has been there!

We need not fear about being real with God. He knows us anyway! We can come to Him in safety. He will help us and heal us. God will come through (Psalm 62:8).

2. The Word of God is our guidebook

Colossians 3:16: *Let the word of Christ richly dwell within you, with all wisdom teaching and admonishing one another with psalms and hymns and spiritual songs, singing with thankfulness in your hearts to God.*

We need to read and meditate regularly on the Word of God. The truth needs to prevail in our lives. God will speak to us through His Word. Trust in His Word and read it daily. Stand on the truth of it. God's Word will work in our lives.

In God's Word there is healing, deliverance, and refreshing. His Word is powerful. The more we fill our minds with His Word, the more our minds will be renewed (Romans 12:2).

We must allow God's Word to work in our lives, and trust His promises to come to pass in our lives. Seek God through His Word and expect Him to speak to us. When he does, we must act on it in obedience. Mix it with faith, so that it is activated in our lives. There is transformation in God's Word. There is renewal and refreshing and challenge. There is everything that we need.

Knowing the truth sets us free!

God can take our disappointments and work them for good. God is trustworthy and unchanging. He is on our side! In the pain of disappointment we can still have faith in God, and listen to Him for guidance and instruction for what He wants for us next. God always wants us to trust Him.

God comforts us and He is our refuge and strength (Psalm 40:1-3).

3. God's promise in disappointment

Psalm 34:10: *The young lions do lack and suffer hunger; But they who seek the Lord shall not be in want of any good thing.*

We lack no good thing. God is a good God Who gives us good things. But when we haven't had answers to prayer in the way we want, it's sometimes harder to believe God's promise. God is good. He is greater than anything else in our lives David found this in Psalm 16:12 – and Paul did too, as he says in Philippians 3:8.

We need to know His love, His presence in our lives. We were made for this. Nothing satisfies us like God does. We were made to know Him, to love Him, to keep company with Him. There is no one else like Him.

Something is good if it brings us nearer to God. Likewise, we need to stay away from things that take us away from God. We have to trust God in what He gives us, and trust Him in what He doesn't give us – it is for our own good.

The three young Hebrew men were put in the fire for not bowing down to the king's statue. They said that God would deliver them – but if He didn't, they would still refuse to bow down! (Daniel 3:18). They trusted God, no matter what. They trusted Him with their lives, and God came through. And a fourth Man showed up in the fire!

4. The Power of Repentance

1 John 1:9: *If we confess our sins, He is faithful and righteous to forgive us our sins and to cleanse us from all unrighteousness.*

If we want things more than we want God, we will be disappointed – because only He truly satisfies us. We bring our disappointments to Him. Repentance is very powerful. If we need to repent because we have put other things first, He will forgive us and cleanse us from all unrighteousness.

We must keep short accounts with God. Watch out for sins in the things we do – sins of deed, and sins in the things we should have done but didn't do. These break the heart of our Heavenly Father. We should only do the things we need to do.

We are created in newness of life in Jesus to do those things that God planned for us (Ephesians 2:10). It's not just a matter of not doing anything *wrong* – we have to do the *right* things. It's not just following rules, it's following Jesus! We are called to follow Him. We need to say yes to Jesus, and walk in obedience to Him in the light. Yes, sometimes there are disappointments and hardships, but God will come through for us

Satan wants us to believe that God is disappointed with us. He wants us to isolate ourselves. He is the Father of lies. God will never disappoint us (Matthew 28:20). God is always with us.

Joseph saw how God turned disappointment for good in his life. His brothers planned something that was meant to harm him. God is always working on our behalf. He has the last word – not Satan, or people, or circumstances. God was with Joseph all the way, through all the disappointments and hurt. We can pour out to God. *For we do not have a high priest who cannot sympathize with our weaknesses, but One who has been tempted in all things as we are, yet without sin* (Hebrews 4:15).

It's good to reflect on how God comes through for us. We need to focus on Him. God plans for our good – always!

5. A God of Restoration

Joel 2:25-26: The Lord says, *"Then I will make up to you for the years That the swarming locust has eaten, The creeping locust, the stripping locust and the gnawing locust, My great army which I sent among you. You will have plenty to eat and be satisfied And praise the name of the Lord your God, Who has dealt wondrously with you; Then My people will never be put to shame."*

God is a God of restoration and abundance. He restored back to Job double! God's plan of salvation is to restore to us everything that we have lost through sin. God can restore ground lost, and sometimes even years lost. He can get back what we have lost. And more!

When David and his men were away fighting, the Amalekites destroyed their homes and took their families captive. First, David's army wept, but then they turned to David for guidance. David asked God what he should do. God said, "Go after them. You will recover everything that was taken from you!" (1 Samuel 30:8).

Satan will attack those close to us in order to get to us. We need to stay alert so we can be aware of this, and come against him. Our strength must always come from God, not from others. David encouraged himself in the Lord. If we want to be discouraged, we will dwell on our problems. If we want to be encouraged, we will focus on God who can solve them. What God did for David, He can do for us!

6. We have authority!

Luke 10:19: *Behold, I have given you authority to tread on serpents and scorpions, and over all the power of the enemy, and nothing will injure you.*

The battle is the Lord's! When the enemy comes with disappointment and discouragement, we have authority over him in Jesus' Name!

David believed that God was bigger than the Giants he faced. Do we believe that? Or does the problem look bigger than God? We can speak to the Giants as David did. "You are coming down in the Name of Jesus, in the Name of the Lord!"

Our words have power. Satan cannot stand God's Word, Christ's blood, and the Name of Jesus! That's the way to get victory over the Giants, just as David did (1 Samuel 17:45-47).

We have Authority in Jesus' Name. His resurrection power is inside every believer. Ephesians 1:18-20: *I pray that the eyes of your heart may be enlightened, so that you will know what is the hope of His calling, what are the riches of the glory of His inheritance in the saints, and what is the surpassing greatness of His power toward us who believe. These are in accordance with the working of the strength of His might which He brought about in Christ, when He raised Him from the dead and seated Him at His right hand in the heavenly places.*

We need to take the Authority God has given us, and use it, and release it. As we do, the enemy is defeated and God moves in power. It's not our own power and authority, it's *His* Power and Authority in us!

Don't give up, keep praying and believing God for victory. Prayer is the powerhouse, the engine room that drives everything else. It is essential in Spiritual Warfare to see the strongholds come down. Pray fervently, with great expectation of what God is going to do. Going over and over our disappointments won't deal with them or solve them. Prayer will! Remember how God has delivered you before. David remembered (1 Samuel 17:37).

God has given us the power the pull down old mental strongholds, wrong ways of thinking (2 Chronicles 10:5). As God's redeemed children, we have the power and authority in us to think as we should, to act as we should, and to speak as we should.

Ephesians 3:20-21: *Now to Him who is able to do far more abundantly beyond all that we ask or think, according to the power that works within us, to Him be the glory in the church and in Christ Jesus to all generations forever and ever. Amen.*

We can do whatever God has told us to do in His Word. We mustn't settle for mediocrity in our walk with God. Here's a quote attributed to Mark Twain: "Twenty years from now you will be more disappointed by the things you didn't do than by the ones you did do. So throw off the bowlines. Sail away from the safe harbour. Catch the trade winds in your sails. Explore. Dream. Discover."

7. Sold out to God

Philippians 3:8-9: *More than that, I count all things to be loss in view of the surpassing value of knowing Christ Jesus my Lord, for whom I have suffered the loss of all things, and count them but rubbish so that I may gain Christ, and may be found in Him, not having a righteousness of my own derived from the Law, but that which is through faith in Christ, the righteousness which comes from God on the basis of faith.*

We need to let go of what we will lose anyway, to gain that which we will never lose. For Paul, he lost every earthly possession. For Job, he had double restored back to him. We can be stripped of the temporal, but we cannot lose the eternal.

Our treasure needs to be in heaven. Eternal things do not fade away. When we put on the altar something that we think we cannot do without, but we know it belongs to God – that's worship. God allowed Abraham to go to the altar, but the sacrifice appeared just as he raised the knife. Sometimes it's just our willingness that God wants – not action. Abraham called this worship. God knew now that Abraham loved Him more than anything else.

We need to be able to pray, telling God that we gladly give Him all it takes for us to be what He wants us to be. We need to give Him our lives, our time, our gifts, our everything. We need to allow Him to remove anything that hinders us from being completely His. Only God completely satisfies us. He is never a disappointment to us. We need to keep seeing the blessings. They are more important than the disappointments that take away our focus, and drain us.

Dale Carnegie wrote:

Two men looked out from prison bars,
One saw the mud, the other saw stars.

What are we focusing on? The mud – or the stars?

God will never let us down! Philippians 4:8-9: *Finally, brethren, whatever is true, whatever is honorable, whatever is right, whatever is pure, whatever is lovely, whatever is of good repute, if there is any excellence and if anything worthy of praise, dwell on these things. The things you have learned and received and heard and seen in me, practice these things, and the God of peace will be with you.*

A Prayer

Help me, Lord Jesus, not to get stuck in disappointment. Help me to find my way forward with You. Help me to keep short accounts with You. Help me to trust in Your promises, and to call on You, and listen to You, and obey You.

Take me from where I am, Lord Jesus, to where You want me to be.

In Jesus' name. Amen.

6. Seven Ways to Walk in Deliverance

From this Chapter

We need to live according to the Spirit, not according to the flesh (Galatians 5:16-17). Jesus set people free from the activity of demons (Luke 6:17-19). We give the enemy access in our lives by believing lies, by wrong behaviour, by bad habits, by unconfessed sin – actions that give Satan room to control us. We need to keep short accounts with God, and keep our lives right, and take back the ground the enemy has stolen from us.

1. Good and evil

Genesis 50:20: Joseph said, *"As for you, you meant evil against me, but God meant it for good in order to bring about this present result, to preserve many people alive."*

We have a realm that we see, and an unseen realm – one for evil and one for good. God is good, Satan is evil and destructive. God's angels are real and good. They protect, guide, prepare the way, minister to believers, and fight the evil realm (Luke 1:26-28). They are powerful (Daniel 10:2-13). They have authority from God.

Demons are also real (Luke 4:41), and powerful (Revelation 16:14). They are always evil and want to destroy (John 10:10). They deceive (John 8:44). They are controlling – but God is the All Powerful One!

His is the greatest power. An angel led Peter out of prison, past the guards to freedom (Acts 12:4-17). We are in a battle. We don't fight flesh and blood, but the powers in the unseen world.

Ephesians 6:12: *For our struggle is not against flesh and blood, but against the rulers, against the powers, against the world forces of this darkness, against the spiritual forces of wickedness in the heavenly places.*

Many disturbing things are happening in the world. Some are caused by natural means, and others are caused by the forces of wickedness in the heavenly places.

2. Believers in Jesus have authority

Ephesians 2:4-6: *But God, being rich in mercy, because of His great love with which He loved us, even when we were dead in our transgressions, made us alive together with Christ (by grace you have been saved), and raised us up with Him, and seated us with Him in the heavenly places in Christ Jesus,*

When we are born again by the Spirit of God, we have authority and power in Jesus Christ. In Matthew 16:19 and Matthew 18:18 we discover we can bind the enemy's activity and free the plans of the Kingdom of God. In James 4:7 we read that as we submit ourselves to God, and resist the devil, he has to flee from us. In the Greek, this means he will run in terror!

Satan and the kingdom of darkness is in opposition to the light of the Kingdom of God (Colossians 1:11-12). In John 10:10 we see how destructive Satan is against all that is of God. But Jesus came to give us abundant life! We have victory in Jesus. He came to destroy the work of Satan (1 John 3:8).

We need to beware of Satan's tactics.1 Peter 5:7-9: *Casting all your anxiety on Him, because He cares for you. Be of sober spirit, be on the alert. Your adversary, the devil, prowls around like a roaring lion, seeking someone to devour. But resist him, firm in your faith, knowing that the same experiences of suffering are being accomplished by your brethren who are in the world.*

3. Jesus moved in His Father's authority

John 8:26: *"I have many things to speak and to judge concerning you, but He who sent Me is true; and the things which I heard from Him, these I speak to the world."*

To be able to move in authority, we have to come under Authority (Matthew 8:7-9). We see an example of this in the account of the Roman officer. He was a man under authority, and also in authority, so he recognised the Authority of Jesus to heal his servant.

We need God's supernatural Power in our lives. We all need to be filled with the Holy Spirit (Ephesians 5:18). We are in a battle with the world, the flesh, and the devil. We cannot serve two masters – the world and God's Kingdom (James 4:4).

We need to live according to the Spirit, not according to the flesh (Galatians 5:16-17). Jesus set people free from the activity of demons (Luke 6:17-19). We give the enemy access in our lives by believing lies, unconfessed sin, and wrong action. We need to keep short accounts with God, and keep our lives right, and take back the ground the enemy has stolen from us.

4. Wrong strongholds hold us back

2 Corinthians 10:3-5: *For though we walk in the flesh, we do not war according to the flesh, for the weapons of our warfare are not of the flesh, but divinely powerful for the destruction of fortresses. We are destroying speculations and every lofty thing raised up against the knowledge of God, and we are taking every thought captive to the obedience of Christ.*

In Romans 7:18-25 we can see how Paul struggled with sin.

But we also see that the answer is in Jesus! Our minds can get captive to sin, but we can be set free through what Jesus has done for us on the cross. He has given us the freedom to choose. We make choices every day. As we focus on God's Word and set our minds on things above, we have life and peace. But setting our minds on the flesh – our old natural desires – is death (Romans 8:6-7).

We can be taken captive by strongholds through wrong thinking. These strongholds oppose God's Truth. A stronghold is a lie that we are believing that affects every area in our lives negatively, and gives the enemy a foothold through sin not dealt with, through anything that opposes God's Truth in His Word.

Strongholds start in our minds with wrong thoughts that become actions, and these can become a hold of the enemy that needs breaking. Any lie we believe is a deception, and Satan is the deceiver. We can believe that God doesn't love us, for example. Then we come out of line with God's Truth in His Word. We need to align our thoughts with the Truth of God's Word in our actions, and in the words we speak.

Our words have the power of life or death in them. They have the power to build up or to put down (Proverbs 18:21).

A curse has no power over us unless we give it that power by agreeing with it, and believing the lie (Proverbs 26:2). If we are fearful of something, there is usually a lie attached to that fear. Deal with the lie in exchange for God's Truth, and realise that fear can go in Jesus' name! Fear is a spirit. God has *not* given us the spirit of fear (2 Timothy 1:7).

5. Stay away from the occult!

Acts 16:16-18: *It happened that as we were going to the place of prayer, a slave-girl having a spirit of divination met us, who was bringing her masters much profit by fortune-telling. Following after Paul and us, she kept crying out, saying, "These men are bond-servants of the Most High God, who are proclaiming to you the way of salvation."*

She continued doing this for many days. But Paul was greatly annoyed, and turned and said to the spirit, "I command you in the name of Jesus Christ to come out of her!" And it came out at that very moment.

Occult means "hidden things." It is supernatural activity which is not related to God the Father, to Jesus or the Holy Spirit. It is not in line with the Word of God (1 Corinthians 8:4-6 and Revelation 22:14-16).

There can be involvement at different levels, through different things, different practices and objects. All these are an inroad for Satan into our lives. We need to believe the truth of God's Word and walk in it.

If we are filled with the Holy Spirit and we want to please God, the Holy Spirit will nudge us about any lies we are believing, and about anything we need to put right in our walk with Him. He loves us too much to leave us where we are!

God is always watching over us to make us more like Jesus every day (Philippians 1:6). If we are aware of sin in our lives, we need to come to God in repentance right away, and put it right with Him and others if we need to. There is great power in repentance when it is true and from our hearts (1 John 1:9). Repentance breaks the enemy's hold on us (Colossians 2:13-15). It is the power of the blood of Jesus. We need to be humble, and submitted to God.

Forgiveness is something we receive, and it must also be something we give to others (Matthew 6:12-15). Repentance is walking in the opposite direction to the sin, so it is also action. We need to have a lifestyle of forgiveness, keeping our hearts right with God.

6. Staying free

Matthew 12:43-45: Jesus said, *"Now when the unclean spirit goes out of a man, it passes through waterless places seeking rest, and does not find it. Then it says, 'I will return to my house from which I came'; and when it comes, it finds it unoccupied, swept, and put in order.*

Then it goes and takes along with it seven other spirits more wicked than itself, and they go in and live there; and the last state of that man becomes worse than the first. That is the way it will also be with this evil generation."

When we are set free, delivered from any evil spirit or any bondage, it is important to walk in that freedom. The door that allowed the wrong spirit or bondage to be there in the first place must be tightly shut. To do this, we must be filled with the presence of God, and filled with the Holy Spirit. If we are filled with the truth and light of God, then we must be sure to shut the door to the enemy.

If we have been delivered, we can and must choose freedom and walk in that freedom. We need to live in our freedom and stay in the blessing of it. We must always be on guard and ready to resist the enemy.

Renewing our minds is an important part of living in freedom (Romans 12:2). Our thoughts are a prime target for the enemy. We need to take any wrong thought captive under the blood of Jesus (2 Corinthians 10:4-5). We are not victims of our thoughts – we have power over them.

Submit to God, resist the devil, draw near to God. As we grow spiritually in our walk with the Lord, we will maintain our freedom. God draws near to us as we draw near to Him. Intimacy with God should always be the most important thing.

7. Scriptures to live by

We need to remember to act on the Word of God, as well as reading it, studying it and standing in faith on its truth. It is true holiness, not legalism, to live our lives in the light of God's Word. The Word of God keeps us from being contaminated with the world. We are *in* the world, but not *of* the world.

Our new nature wants to obey God. The more we feed it, the more it will grow and dominate our lives. 1 John 3:8-9: *The one who practices sin is of the devil; for the devil has sinned from the beginning. The Son of God appeared for this purpose, to destroy the works of the devil. No one who is born of God practices sin, because His seed abides in him; and he cannot sin, because he is born of God.*

Colossians 1:13-14: *For He rescued us from the domain of darkness, and transferred us to the kingdom of His beloved Son, in whom we have redemption, the forgiveness of sins.*

There is only one way to expose Satan's schemes and defeat them – by making sure we walk closely with God, studying and acting on the Word of God, and staying close in prayer. This is how we guard against the enemy's tactics. Our character is revealed by the choices we make every day, walking in the Light as He is in the Light. In Him there is no darkness at all!

Ephesians 6:11-13: *Put on the full armor of God, so that you will be able to stand firm against the schemes of the devil. For our struggle is not against flesh and blood, but against the rulers, against the powers, against the world forces of this darkness, against the spiritual forces of wickedness in the heavenly places. Therefore, take up the full armor of God, so that you will be able to resist in the evil day, and having done everything, to stand firm.*

Romans 16:20: *The God of peace will soon crush Satan under your feet. The grace of our Lord Jesus be with you.*

A Prayer

Help me, Lord Jesus, to live and walk in Your freedom, that I may recognise the authority I have in Your Name, and use it against the enemy.

Help me to walk in Your Spirit and not in the flesh, to keep short accounts with You and live right before You, doing the things that please You and agree with Your Word.

Help me to walk in Your Truth, and fill me with Your Holy Spirit.

In Jesus' Name. Amen.

7. Seven Truths about Communication

From this Chapter

We were created by God to communicate with Him and with each other. Communication is more than just talking. There are many ways that we were made to communicate. Our communication with others is always affected by our own communication with God, just as is everything else in our lives. We need to communicate the truth of the gospel to people, but always in love.

1. Good communication is motivated by love

Galatians 5:22-23: *But the fruit of the Spirit is love, joy, peace, patience, kindness, goodness, faithfulness, gentleness, self-control; against such things there is no law.*

Genuine communication is produced by the Holy Spirit, by the fruit of the Spirit. We were created by God to communicate with Him and with each other. Communication is more than just talking. There are many ways that we were made to communicate. Psalm 139:14 says that we are *fearfully and wonderfully made*!

Jesus, on the cross dying for our sins to bring us back to God, is God communicating with us, telling us that He wants to restore relationship and communication with mankind through His Only Son. This also brings us together in the Body of Christ.

Jesus shows us that the key to genuine communication is found in the heart. It goes deeper than speaking and listening to each other, although that is a large part of it. But if it is not in the heart, then it is empty.

Jesus said, *"You brood of vipers, how can you, being evil, speak what is good? For the mouth speaks out of that which fills the heart"* (Matthew 12:34). What comes out of our mouths shows what is in our hearts – and what is in our hearts affects our communication negatively or positively.

Our communication with each other is always affected by our own communication with God, just as is everything else in our lives. We need to communicate the truth of the gospel to people, but always in love.

Matthew 28:18-20: *And Jesus came up and spoke to them, saying, "All authority has been given to Me in heaven and on earth. Go therefore and make disciples of all the nations, baptizing them in the name of the Father and the Son and the Holy Spirit, teaching them to observe all that I commanded you; and lo, I am with you always, even to the end of the age."*

Our communication ought to be motivated by compassion and love, and with a real concern for people's well-being (Matthew 9:36).

We should always speak the truth in love (Ephesians 4:15). If we love people, sometimes we have to confront things, but it should always be done out of the heart of love. Real love, God's love, does not sweep things under the carpet or ignore things that need to be brought to the light in the right way for everyone's good. Likewise, when someone needs to speak to us for our good, we need to receive it in the right way and act on it. They are doing us a favour! If it's given in love, receive it! (Psalm 141:5).

2. We need to be humble

Philippians 2:3-4: *Do nothing from selfishness or empty conceit, but with humility of mind regard one another as more important than yourselves; do not merely look out for your own personal interests, but also for the interests of others.*

We need to communicate with humility. Pride is a massive blockage to true communication. Pride will keep us from being real and open with each other. It will cause our communication to be self-centred. Good communication is humble and self-sacrificing.

We need to build each other up by being gracious and encouraging, and not gossiping. James 1:19-20 tells us to be quick to listen, slow to speak, and slow to become angry. We will not be able to communicate in the way God wants us to, if we do it in our own strength or self effort. It has to be in His power (John 15:5).

We need to communicate in the power of the Holy Spirit, not in the flesh – in other words, not following our natural desires that work against God. We should watch our communication and the words we use. They have power (Proverbs 18:21).

We need to be aware of the feelings behind our words, and our tone of voice. We also need to be aware that our motives are good, and for the other person's good. We need to think before we speak. We need to be wise with our words (Titus 3:2).

Good communication involves good talking, good listening, and being attentive! Our words should bless those who hear them. They should bless, lift, and encourage. Communication needs to be positive. Ephesians 4:29: *Let no unwholesome word proceed from your mouth, but only such a word as is good for edification according to the need of the moment, so that it will give grace to those who hear.*

3. Poor communication

Galatians 5:25-26: *If we live by the Spirit, let us also walk by the Spirit. Let us not become boastful, challenging one another, envying one another.*

We may come up against someone who finds it hard to express themselves, and that can be hard for the listener. We need to be patient in communicating with them. We may sense that they are struggling with fear, or jealousy, or unforgiveness for example.

We never know what others are going through, so we need to be loving and patient in our communication with them. It can cause any of us to struggle if we don't renew our minds daily in the Word of God, and walk in the Spirit.

Sometimes we can come across negative communication that is not helpful, and we may feel kept in the dark. These negatives are usually there because people are not seeing communication in God's way, but from an earthly point of view, and not by the Spirit of God. This can happen to any of us if we feed our old nature, and don't renew our minds daily with God's Word. The longer we dwell on the things of the flesh – our earthly desires – the more they will control us.

We need good communication in every area of our lives. Many marriages fail because of poor, and sometimes no communication. There can be many problems caused in church fellowship life and relationships through lack of communication. The same applies to the workplace, and families, and neighbours – the list is endless. Good communication is vital in our lives. In these days when there is so much technology, it's so easy to opt out of really good, strong communication with each other.

As Christians, one thing that especially affects every other communication in our lives is our spiritual walk with God, and our communication with Him. The effects of this go far and wide. The ripples go out further and further. If this area is lacking, so will every other area be lacking – not just good communication.

Good communication is not an automatic thing. We need to listen to the voice of the Holy Spirit in our lives, and obey Him. He will lead us the right way, and give us what we need to be good communicators in His love, using the attributes of the fruit of the Holy Spirit.

4. Over-busyness

1 Kings 20:40: *"While your servant was busy here and there, he was gone."*

We can be too busy to communicate in the right way. We can be over-committed doing things that God never intended us to do! We need to have the time to care, the time to show love to people, the time to "be there" for them when the Holy Spirit prompts us. That is why it is so important to build a life of prayer and listening to Him. *And* doing what he says!

We need to come into alignment with God, and He will never over-stretch us. He never puts too much on us so that we are overburdened and so caught up that we have no time to respond to the needs of others. His yoke is easy (Matthew 11:30). We are all running in a race, but if we see someone has fallen, do we stop and help them up, or just keep running? Galatians 6:1-2).

We need to value our time and use it wisely, making the most of it. We need to make our time count. We need to get rid of the things God never gave us to do, and use our time wisely doing what He has given us to do. If our schedule is out of control, then we need to seek God's help. We must not allow ourselves to be pressured by the demands of people, but we must listen to God and His plan.

We always need to have the time for others, especially if they are hurting in some way. We need time to communicate God's acceptance and love for them, as they are, refusing to give up on them because of what His great grace can work in their lives through us. We also need to be asking God for the wisdom that we need.

5. Love is patient and kind

Colossians 3:12: *So, as those who have been chosen of God, holy and beloved, put on a heart of compassion, kindness, humility, gentleness and patience.*

Good communication is patient and kind. Lovingkindness is

tactful in dealing with others. "Tact" means "to touch." We need to be sensitive to other people's feelings. There are wise ways of being tactful in our communication, without being hurtful or damaging.

God will give us the delicate, sensitive touch with others – if we ask Him. Being tactful and wise in our communication makes all the difference in helping the other person to respond to us and to God (2 Peter 1:5-7).

When we feel cared about and loved, this encourages good communication because it brings out the best in us. We need to feel accepted, loved, and understood. This is the heart of God, even when He is dealing with us. The enemy will do all he can to destroy this kind of communication. He knows how powerful it is. He knows how we can develop and grow spiritually in the atmosphere of love, acceptance and encouragement with each other.

The enemy does not want unity in the body of Christ, and he does his best to cause mistrust and misunderstanding among us. We need to be aware of his schemes, and make sure we don't give him an open door of opportunity – united we stand, divided we fall!

Poor communication gives the devil a foothold in our relationships with one another. When Roman soldiers went into battle, they locked their shields together to form a strong barrier to keep out the weapons of the enemy. They knew the truth of the power and strength of standing together in battle against the enemy (Psalm 133:1 and Ephesians 4:3).

6. We need to keep our conscience clear

Acts 23:1: *Paul, looking intently at the Council, said, "Brethren, I have lived my life with a perfectly good conscience before God up to this day."*

We need to be living with a clean conscience before God. When our conscience is led by the truth of God's Word, it will lead us to do the right thing. If we ignore it, then our conscience can become hardened over the years, and that will cause us to compromise with sin.

If we want the blessing of God in our lives, we must respond and keep our conscience right before God. In Acts 24:16 Paul tells how he tries with all his strength to keep a clean conscience before God and man.

In our walk with God, we need to do what only we can do, and then God will do what only He can do. We need to be committed to spiritual growth, to bringing forth good fruit in our lives. If we try in our own strength, we will fail every time. It is the power of His Spirit living through us that we need (Zechariah 4:6).

The battle is not ours, but God's. We need to stand in faith, and let God's Spirit flow through us. We don't become Christians by trying to be perfect, or striving and trying our best to live right! Salvation is a free gift – we don't earn it. *For by grace you have been saved through faith; and that not of yourselves, it is the gift of God; not as a result of works, so that no one may boast* (Ephesians 5:8-9).

Jesus won the victory for us on the cross! It is a *gift*! Through Him and His life within us, we can be all that He wants us to be. There is nothing lacking with Him. In Him we have everything we need for life and holiness.

As people of character who have the Holy Spirit's attributes, we are abiding in the Vine, drawing power and strength my close connection to the Vine (Jesus), obeying God, trusting in His strength, studying, reading and relying on His Word, spending quality time in God's presence and listening to His voice as we communicate daily with Him. If we do this, communication will affect our lives and the lives of other people for good, and for God.

7. Above and beyond!

Ephesians 3:20-21: *Now to Him who is able to do far more abundantly beyond all that we ask or think, according to the power that works within us, to Him be the glory in the church and in Christ Jesus to all generations forever and ever. Amen.*

He is a God of abundance! We must not underestimate what God can do through His Spirit. We have the Kingdom of God living in us. What an amazing thing! We weren't called just to survive, but to rule and to reign. We are *more* than conquerors (Romans 8:37)!

We have the same power in us that the disciples had in them. They stood out. We need to be determined to tap into the power of the Kingdom within us, in every area of our lives. We have Resurrection Power in us!

The more we grow in hearing God and acting on the Holy Spirit's leading, the more we will move and grow in our God-given Authority and Power. We need to think, act, and speak according to the truths of the Word of God.

We need to stir up the fruit of the Holy Spirit in our lives, to express God's love to others, to show others that they are valued and precious to us *and* to God. We need to go the extra mile, to give and forgive. We need to bless others at every chance we get.

We need to practise good communication, speak positive words of encouragement, and act out of compassion. If we always wait until we feel like it, we will never do it! It's not about feelings. It's about the self-discipline needed to stir it up within us. We can *always* find ways to bless others. If we want more of God, then we need to give to others what we have received from Him. Then, what we give away will increase!

We need to believe in ourselves – not in our own ability, but in what God has placed within us. The Power of the Kingdom of God! We are the Kingdom of God on earth. Salt and light. Let us shine in the darkness, and bring glory and honour to God!

A Prayer

Help me, Lord Jesus, to be a good communicator, and to walk in Your Holy Spirit, and bring forth good fruit. Help me to love with Your love. May I spend quality time in Your presence, hearing You and obeying You.

Help me to encourage others in You, and be sensitive to the needs of others. Help me only to do those things that You want me to do. Give me a fresh revelation of who I am in You, and of the power within me.

In Jesus' Name. Amen.

8. Seven Truths about Authentic Christianity

From this Chapter

If we talk Godly talk, we should walk a Godly walk! What we claim to believe should have everything to do with how we behave. We need to be true and trustworthy. We need to be real. We need to do what we say. We still have faults and failings, but if we are real we are aware that God is dealing with them as we allow Him to. None of us is perfect, but in that imperfection we can still be authentic. We are perfect in Christ!

1. Faith in Jesus Christ through the gospel

John 3:16: *"For God so loved the world, that He gave His only begotten Son, that whoever believes in Him shall not perish, but have eternal life."*

Anyone who has genuine faith in Jesus understands and believes the truth of the Gospel. We will confess that Jesus Christ is Lord. That doesn't mean we will never sin if we are a Christian, but we will not want to go into sin wilfully on a continuous basis (1 John 4:15).

We will not want to do anything that displeases God – we will want to please Him. And if we do sin, and confess our sin as soon as we can, we will want to keep short accounts with God. We will know deep down inside that something we are doing is wrong (1 John 3:9).

We will enjoy fellowship with other Christians and want to be with them (1 John 5:1). God's plan for us was never isolation. We need each other in the body of Christ. We cannot survive alone as a Christian. We need the encouragement of others around us (Hebrews 10:24-25).

2. We will want to obey God

1 John 5:3: *For this is the love of God, that we keep His commandments; and His commandments are not burdensome.*

If we are a true follower of Jesus we will want to walk in obedience to His commands. We will not want to fit into the world, and we will not want to do our own thing.

God's laws are for our good – they are not there to restrict us or make us miserable. They are for our protection. If we are always breaking the commands of God, then we don't love Him (1 John 1:6).

If we really know Him and love Him, we will not want to fit into the world in any way. We will want our lives to be a testimony of God's blessing and goodness, so that others can know him too (Romans 12:2 and 1 John 2:15).

If we are a true Christian, we will love and obey the Word of God (1 John 2:5). We cannot live the Christian life effectively without loving God's Word. It is His message to us. It is our guidebook in our lives.

If we are a true disciple of Jesus, if we really love Him, then we will read and study the Word of God. We will live by the truth of it (2 Timothy 3:16). The Word of God is living and active, and is powerful in our daily lives. It is our mirror for life, showing us where we are and what we need to do about it. If we love God we will act on His Word.

We need His Word daily. It's the only way to grow and develop in God.

3. The fruit it produces

Colossians 1:3-5: *We give thanks to God, the Father of our Lord Jesus Christ, praying always for you, since we heard of your faith in Christ Jesus and the love which you have for all the saints; because of the hope laid up for you in heaven, of which you previously heard in the word of truth.*

Paul writes in this Scripture about the fruit of Christianity – the fruit of faith in Jesus Christ. It is the fruit of love for other believers, and the fruit of the hope of Heaven.

If we talk Godly talk, we should walk a Godly walk! What we claim to believe should have everything to do with how we behave. We need to be true and trustworthy. We need to be real. We need to do what we say.

We still have faults and failings, but if we are real we are aware that God is dealing with them as we allow Him to. None of us is perfect, but in that imperfection we can still be authentic. We are perfect in Christ! (2 Corinthians 5:21).

Authenticity is transparency and being willing to admit failure. It's the rejection of pretence and hypocrisy. It's truth filling all areas of life, being open and real.

Without Christ we can do nothing (John 15:5). But do we admit that this is true in our lives? That we are helpless without the Holy Spirit working in us and through us? It's not us, it's Him in us and through us – the Life and Power of Jesus Christ

Galatians 2:20: *I have been crucified with Christ; and it is no longer I who live, but Christ lives in me; and the life which I now live in the flesh I live by faith in the Son of God, who loved me and gave Himself up for me.*

What a promise!

4. We have to "put off" and "put on"

Ephesians 4:21-24: *if indeed you have heard Him and have been taught in Him, just as truth is in Jesus, that, in reference to your former manner of life, you lay aside the old self, which is being corrupted in accordance with the lusts of deceit, and that you be renewed in the spirit of your mind, and put on the new self, which in the likeness of God has been created in righteousness and holiness of the truth.*

We have to "put off" the old nature and "put on" the new nature in Christ, to clothe ourselves with our new nature. And *we* have to do this. God won't do it for us, because He has already made us brand-new creations in Him!

It's good to be humble and honest, and know that God is working in us to make us more and more like Him. Humility is so important, and we need to make sure we don't become proud in any way. Always remember where God took us from, so we stay thankful to Him. We must not think too highly of ourselves in the wrong way.

In Matthew 7:15-23 we read about good fruit not coming from a rotten tree. And in verse 20, we read that rotten fruit doesn't come from a good tree. We are identified by the fruit we produce. Verse 22 talks about the Judgement, and all that we can do and *still* not know him, because our deeds are evil.

We are not known by our gifts, but by the fruit of our character. The real key of everything is that we obey our Father in Heaven. Verse 21 says that obedience is better than sacrifice. See also 1 Samuel 15:22.

5. Satan's plan is to trip us up!

1 Corinthians 10:12: *Therefore let him who thinks he stands take heed that he does not fall.*

This verse warns us to be aware of Satan's devices. He can tell us lies, and convince us that we will never fall, so we get deceived into thinking we are too strong to fall. This verse warns us to "take heed" to be aware of his lies. If we listen to them, then he can trap us into being deceived about ourselves, and start to trust in our own strength.

We need to be aware of pride that goes before a fall. Satan loves to get us focused on spiritually strong people who fall, and tells us *we* will never make it! But we have God's promise in Jude 24 that He is able to keep us from stumbling. But it's in *His* strength, not ours. That is why there is no room for pride, *or* for feeling inadequate!

Paul said, *"When I am weak then I am strong"* (2 Corinthians 12:10). God's power is perfected in our weakness (2 Corinthians 12:9). We are living letters, read by all men (2 Corinthians 3:2). People are watching to see if we are hypocrites.

God doesn't hide any of the shortcomings or failures of the "saints" – the name in the Bible for *all* Christians! (1 Corinthians 10:11-12). These words are written down so we can learn from them, and find encouragement knowing that God does not give up on us. So we must not want to give up if we stumble. We need to repent, and put it right with God and others if we need to, and receive His forgiveness. Then we need to forgive ourselves, learn from what we have done, and move on! (1 John 1:9).

6. Put God first

Luke 12:31: *But seek His kingdom, and these things will be added to you.*

God wants to be Number One in our lives. He wants us to seek His Kingdom *first*. Jesus always put his Father's agenda first (John 8:29). We need to take time to bring our day to the Father, and know what He is saying to us today. How is He leading us? God wants the first fruit of our day – not the left-overs. He wants the best part of our day. He wants *all* of our lives!

We need His presence in our lives more than anything else. His presence makes all the difference (Exodus 33:14-16). Other people see the difference when we have the presence of God. They may not always know what it is, but they sense something different.

Moses didn't want to go if God's presence didn't go with him. As we trust God, and allow the Holy Spirit to guide us along, He will show us the best pathway for our lives.

Jesus spent much time talking to His Father in prayer. Our communication with God should always be of Number One importance in our day – praying, and listening, and expecting to hear. In Matthew 6:5-8 we are warned not to be like the hypocrites when we are praying, but to be real in our prayer. Not trying to impress others, and staying away from repetition. God knows what we need even before we ask. Verse 9 of Matthew 6 is the Lord 's Prayer, the prayer Jesus taught His disciples.

So when we pray, it is to our Father –whether we are in the secret place or the prayer meeting. We are not to make a show of how spiritual we are, but we should pray in faith with great expectation!

7. Not conformed but transformed!

Romans 12:2: *And do not be conformed to this world, but be transformed by the renewing of your mind, so that you may prove what the will of God is, that which is good and acceptable and perfect.*

As believers we have the *greatest* power living in us (1 John 4:4). The Spirit living within us helps us to resist the pressures of the world. God's plan for us, as true believers, is total transformation. As we see in Romans 12:1 we are to come as "living sacrifices" on the altar for God. Is this too much to ask?

When we think of what He has done for us, it's a day by day yielding everything to God. It's a daily dying to our self-life, and living for Him.

We need to refuse to allow our old nature to take over and rule, or we will reap sin. If we feed our new nature, we will reap much blessing. Whichever nature we feed, that one will dominate. It is an act of worship. It is surrendered hearts and lives. What is in our surrendered heart will bring us joy! Authenticity is not just going through the motions. Our hearts have to be in it.

Prayer is an act of worship from our hearts. Our response to God should be out of love, not fear. He is not shaking His fist at us, and threatening to punish us if we don't surrender. God's grace is a free gift. His love is unconditional (Romans 5:8).

If we conform to this world, that is a choice we have made.

This choice will allow the enemy to rob us of our freedom in Christ, opening a door to bondage. When we make the right choice, the door is opened to transformation by God's Power. Transformation happens daily as we commit ourselves to the renewing of our minds, thinking God's thoughts through the Word of God, instead of thoughts that belong to the old nature.

Jesus' sacrifice on the cross made it possible for us to choose the right way. Our sinful nature was dealt with on the cross. It died so we can be alive to God. Sin need never again be our master. We have the freedom to choose, and to live in newness of life! (Romans 6:5-14).

A prayer

Help me, Lord, to be a true Christian, to live as I should live, to talk the talk and walk the walk so that my life will bring glory to You. Make me a living sacrifice acceptable to You.

In Jesus' Name. Amen.

9. Seven Truths about Spiritual Warfare

From this Chapter

God is real. The devil is real. Spiritual warfare is part of our Christian life – we are in a battle! If we allow anything of our old nature to control us, we will be living in defeat in the battle. We can ignore it and be in denial of it, but we still live in defeat. We must remember that victory or defeat touches every area of our lives.

1. We can live in victory!

Romans 8:37: *But in all these things we overwhelmingly conquer through Him who loved us.*

God is real. The devil is real. Spiritual warfare is part of our

Christian life – we are in a battle! If we allow anything of our old nature to control us, we will be living in defeat in the battle. We can ignore it and be in denial of it, but we still live in defeat. We must remember that victory or defeat touches every area of our lives.

We cannot grow spiritually if we are not walking in obedience in an area that God has been speaking to us about. One step of obedience leads to another step in our spiritual walk. The enemy will find a way of making us feel overwhelmed and unable to cope. God always gives us what we need to overcome in the battle.

We can open our own doors to allow the enemy to defeat us. If he can get us into denial and making excuses, he will control us. And that will affect every area of our lives.

God doesn't ask us to do something that He hasn't already given us the ability and power to do. Philippians 1:6: *For I am confident of this very thing, that He who began a good work in you will perfect it until the day of Christ Jesus.*

In Romans 7:23-25 Paul thanks God who gives us the victory through our Lord Jesus Christ!

2. Seeing the spiritual battle for what it is

James 4:7: *Submit therefore to God. Resist the devil and he will flee from you.*

The first step to overcoming is to see the battle for what it really is. When we recognise that, we will deal with it. The enemy loves to keep us unaware and ignorant of his actions. He blinds our eyes to the truth. The Word of God tells us that knowing the truth makes us free! (John 8:32).

Every day we are in a battle with an enemy who wants to keep us in defeat. We need to use the power of the Word of God against him. We need to wear our armour and use our weapons – prayer, praise, the Word of God, and regular fellowship.

We need to guard our hearts and renew our minds with the Word of God daily. When we submit to God's Authority, we can resist the enemy and he will flee from us. Freedom and victory is a walk and a way of life. Don't let sin control, but leave the lesser things behind.

Serve God. Confess any sin. Reject pride, rebellion, and our self-life. Forgive others. Humble ourselves and ask for forgiveness. Don't give the enemy any inroad. Renounce doubt and unbelief, and any fear – anything else that needs renouncing. Bind and rebuke all related spirits in Jesus' name! (Romans 10:17).

Stand on the Word of God in faith. Perfect peace comes in staying focused on God and His Word (Isaiah 26:3). We need to learn to live in the victory of our freedom. It's a lifestyle, and it's vitally important. It's our responsibility to have a strong spiritual life, built around God's presence and His Word. We can speak the Word of God out loud and resist the enemy. The Word of God is active and sharper than a two-edged sword (James 4:7).

If we have been set free from something, the enemy will always try to trap us again through temptation and sin. The enemy needs to have our permission or our carelessness to gain a foothold into our lives. We must not give him any place (Ephesians 4:17).

If the enemy does break through, we must immediately confess our failure, and take a strong stand against him. Resist and refuse him in Jesus' name. Submitting to God and resisting the enemy spells victory!

3. The power of God's Word

Hebrews 4:12: *For the word of God is living and active and sharper than any two-edged sword, and piercing as far as the division of soul and spirit, of both joints and marrow, and able to judge the thoughts and intentions of the heart.*

The Word of God is our most powerful weapon. In Luke 4 we read how Jesus dealt with the enemy in His temptation in the wilderness. Jesus pointed him to the Scriptures three times. We need to read and study the Word of God – *and* act on it. We defeat the enemy through God's truth (2 Corinthians 10:3-5).

A wrong stronghold is anything that needs to come under God's Authority. Strongholds are the lies of the enemy. These lies can become strongholds in our lives if they are not exposed and dealt with according to the Word of God.

The enemy is the father of lies. We need to take every wrong thought captive under the blood of Jesus in obedience to Him. The Word of God tells us what to fill our minds with (Philippians 4:8).

4. The enemy knows our weaknesses

Isaiah 54:17: *"No weapon that is formed against you will prosper; And every tongue that accuses you in judgment you will condemn. This is the heritage of the servants of the Lord, And their vindication is from Me," declares the Lord.*

Weapons are formed against us as the children of God, but they will not defeat us! The attacks usually begin in our thought patterns. The enemy knows what to attack us with – and when (Ephesians 6:11-17).

We need to be aware, but not to fear or cower. We need to stand strong and be aware that Satan is under our feet, and we have the victory in Jesus Christ. God has raised us up to sit with Him in the Heavenly Places. We need to recognise and maintain our firm position in Christ.

The enemy is out to do three things: to kill, steal, and destroy (John 10:10). He never plays fair. He will attack every area of our lives. He knows our weak spots, and pushes them to the limit. We need to use our weapons and push back – to wield the sword of the Spirit, the Word of God (Ephesians 6:17).

God fights for us! The more we win the victory in different areas of our lives, the stronger and bolder we become in God (Romans 16:20).

5. Be watchful

1 Peter 5:8: *Be of sober spirit, be on the alert. Your adversary, the devil, prowls around like a roaring lion, seeking someone to devour.*

We must not allow the enemy to trick us into relying on our feelings instead of on the Word of God. The enemy wants to affect our words, our ways and thoughts, so we become vulnerable to believe his lies. He prowls like a lion, seeking whom he can devour. He never gives up!

We need to be watching and praying, and wearing our armour, depending only on the Word of God. In Jesus, the battle and the victory are won! When Jesus died on the cross, He won the victory *totally* over all principalities and evil powers, as he cried, *"It is finished!"* (John 19:30). The work of salvation was totally completed, once and for all.

1 John 5:4: *For whatever is born of God overcomes the world; and this is the victory that has overcome the world – our faith.*

6. The power of prayer

Romans 8:26: *In the same way the Spirit also helps our weakness; for we do not know how to pray as we should, but the Spirit Himself intercedes for us with groanings too deep for words.*

The enemy wants to rob us of our joy and our peace, and bring fear and a sense of hopelessness. He plays on the "What Ifs?" – especially about the future. We need to allow the Holy Spirit to pray and intercede through us.

He will lead us and guide us in prayer. He will prompt us what to pray for – and how. Prayer changes things radically. As we pray, Heaven gets busy as transactions take place in the Heavenlies while the power of prayer is released.

As we pray in the mighty Name of Jesus, we release the power of God into situations that will turn them for good. God's Power is the *Greatest Power!* And His Power *lives in us*. We have been given *authority* in prayer. We need to be confident in this, so that we can pray in faith, *believing*!

7. How big is our God?

1 Samuel 17:47: David said to the Philistines, "... *that all this assembly may know that the Lord does not deliver by sword or by spear; for the battle is the Lord's and He will give you into our hands."*

How we cope with life and warfare depends on how big our God is. If we see God as too small, we will be anxious, worried and fearful, and unable to trust Him. We will find it hard to feel accepted, loved, and forgiven. We will not see Him as He is – All Powerful and in control. Then we feel vulnerable and open to anything that comes our way.

If we see God as too small, we will not be confident in who we are, and in our position in Him. This means we will be unable to pray in faith, with the assurance that God hears us and will answer us. Without knowing the acceptance and love of a loving Heavenly Father, we will become people-pleasers, and listen more to their opinion of us, rather than believing how God sees us.

When we know how big God *really* is, we can face anything in His strength, knowing He will not let us down – knowing that the battle is His! John Newton said, “If the Lord be with us, we have no cause of fear. His eye is upon us, His arm over us, His ear open to our prayer – His grace sufficient, His promise unchangeable.”

Prayer

Help me, Lord Jesus, to stand strong in You in the battle. Help me to live in Your victory, and know who I am in You. Help me to obey You step-by-step, gaining ground in my walk with You.

Help me to stand in faith on Your Word, and wear my armour and use my weapons. I submit myself to You, and will, with Your help, apply Your truth to my life.

I will not allow the enemy’s lies to control me in any way. Help me to recognise and maintain my position in You, and pray in faith, believing.

In Jesus’ Name. Amen.

10. Seven Truths about Kindness

From this Chapter

We must not belittle the fruit of kindness. It brings people together to find common ground. In hard situations and differing opinions, kindness is the way to walk. It helps every situation and relationship in life. It helps us relate to those who are different to us. Kindness calls us to sacrifice our own comfort zone, not just by using kind words, but by action too. Kindness is a lifestyle. We need to ask God to strengthen kindness in our lives. His kindness is supernatural.

1. Kindness is underrated

Philemon 1:7: *For I have come to have much joy and comfort in your love, because the hearts of the saints have been refreshed through you, brother.*

We underestimate the power of kindness. It is powerful, radical – and sometimes risk-taking. Kindness is powerful to change lives! (Romans 2:4).

Kindness can break down barriers and bring people together in love. It can heal and restore relationships. It can bring leaders together, and families, and also nations! Its strength can move mountains!

We must not belittle the fruit of kindness. It brings people together to find common ground. In hard situations and differing opinions, kindness is the way to walk. It helps every situation and relationship in life. It helps us relate to those who are different to us.

Kindness calls us to sacrifice our own comfort zone, not just by using kind words, but by action too. Kindness is a lifestyle. We need to ask God to strengthen kindness in our lives.

In Matthew 25:35-40, Jesus tells us that when we do acts of kindness to others, we are doing them to Him. It's a biblical way of life.

2. Kindness is supernatural

2 Corinthians 6:6: ... *in purity, in knowledge, in patience, in kindness, in the Holy Spirit, in genuine love.*

Kindness is supernatural in its acts and attitudes to other people, even when they don't deserve it and don't appreciate it. Kindness is unconditional, and it is towards our enemies as well as our family and friends. Luke 6:35 Jesus says, *"But love your enemies, and do good, and lend, expecting nothing in return; and your reward will be great, and you will be sons of the Most High; for He Himself is kind to ungrateful and evil men."*

Our kindness comes from the heart of our Father (Ephesians 4:32). Jesus was sometimes kind in a rebuking way, for the good of others. So kindness may not always be easy to take!

Jesus is kind enough not to leave us where we are, so we

should follow His example for the good of each other. The kindness that comes from God is not natural – it is undeserved. It is not conditional.

It's not natural to love and show kindness to those who have wronged us in any way. It is *supernatural.* It has nothing to do with our own goodness – it's the fruit of His kindness within us, through the Holy Spirit. Kindness is produced in us by the Spirit of God (Galatians 5:22).

The gospel is about the supernatural love and kindness of God in Jesus our Saviour. It is not by anything we have done. We have been justified by His grace, which is the free gift of God.

Titus 3:4-5: *But when the kindness of God our Savior and His love for mankind appeared, He saved us, not on the basis of deeds which we have done in righteousness, but according to His mercy, by the washing of regeneration and renewing by the Holy Spirit,*

3. Kindness is very powerful

Proverbs 11:17: *The merciful man does himself good, But the cruel man does himself harm.*

Are we kind? How do we talk about others? Are we kind or critical? We need to be aware that what is in our heart overflows into speech. We need to watch our words. Kindness is love in action. Kindness is a choice of being kind to others, as well as being kind to ourselves.

Kindness is the fruit of the Spirit of God within us. We need to teach our children to be kind, and to bless others. Kindness shows others that God is at work in our lives. It cannot be false, because it is from our heart through the Holy Spirit. It's much more than being nice and agreeable. It is always for the good of others.

Kindness is strong against the plans and purposes of the enemy. It brings peace when there could be division. It brings unity, healing, and restoration in relationships. It takes the sting out of miscommunication and misunderstanding. It is like healing ointment on a sore or running wound.

Never underestimate the supernatural power of kindness at

work in a believer's life. It comes from the very heart of God Himself. Let the fruit of kindness be demonstrated through the Church to a needy world, so it flows within the body of Christ – and the ripples flow out, reaching far and wide.

4. Examples of kindness

Luke 10:30-34: Jesus said, *"A man was going down from Jerusalem to Jericho, and fell among robbers, and they stripped him and beat him, and went away leaving him half dead. And by chance a priest was going down on that road, and when he saw him, he passed by on the other side.*

"Likewise a Levite also, when he came to the place and saw him, passed by on the other side. But a Samaritan, who was on a journey, came upon him; and when he saw him, he felt compassion, and came to him and bandaged up his wounds, pouring oil and wine on them; and he put him on his own beast, and brought him to an inn and took care of him."

The Samaritan went the extra mile. He not only stopped, he followed it through. It was in his heart. He could have passed by. But instead of passing by, he not only stopped but helped the man by binding up his wounds. He then took him to an inn where he looked after him all night. What kindness!

In Luke 5:18-20 we see the story of the paralysed man. When his friends let him down to the roof at Jesus' feet, Jesus immediately responded to their faith. The man's sins were forgiven and he was healed! An act of kindness changed this man's life for ever, and it was something he would never forget. Ephesians 4:32: *Be kind to one another, tender-hearted, forgiving each other, just as God in Christ also has forgiven you.*

In Genesis 24:19 Abraham sends his servant out to find a wife for his son Isaac. As his servant stood by a well in a small town, he prayed to God that the woman who offered to water his camels would be God's chosen one. Rebekah comes along, and offers to do this (the 13-14).

Rebekah wasn't aware that the simple act of kindness would lead to such blessing in her life. She was generous to someone she didn't even know. She was giving freely in her serving –

unconditionally. She went above and beyond (Matthew 5:41). And what a blessing she received!

5. God's lovingkindness

Colossians 3:12: *So, as those who have been chosen of God, holy and beloved, put on a heart of compassion, kindness, humility, gentleness and patience.*

God loves us with an everlasting love. With lovingkindness He has drawn us to Himself (Jeremiah 31:3). The psalmist realised this in Psalm 63:3-4: *Because Your lovingkindness is better than life, My lips will praise You. So I will bless You as long as I live; I will lift up my hands in Your name.*

It's good to be thankful to God, and recall His lovingkindness to us! It's not what we deserve or earn – it's unconditionally lavished upon us.

Psalm 69:16: *Answer me, O Lord, for Your lovingkindness is good; According to the greatness of Your compassion, turn to me.*

It's good to be thankful when we pray. It's an expression of faith and expectancy in a loving, kind, gracious God. Let's remember to be thankful. Because of the kindness we have received, we need to practise being kind. We need to clothe ourselves with kindness, just as people notice what we wear. They will notice our attitudes. Kindness will always be noticed. It's good to live in an attitude of gratitude to God.

6. Treat our enemies with kindness

Proverbs 25:21-22: *If your enemy is hungry, give him food to eat; And if he is thirsty, give him water to drink; For you will heap burning coals on his head, And the Lord will reward you.*

If we belong to Jesus, it's not good to simply ignore our enemies. We need to actively show them love and kindness. As it says in these verses in Proverbs, if they are hungry – feed them. If they are thirsty – give them a drink. We have a choice how we treat our enemies. With kindness, or with retaliation?

If we are not showing kindness, then what we profess to believe is dead. Our faith needs to be active (James 2:14-17). We need to show kindness at every chance we get. We must never get so busy that we can't stop when we need to show kindness to someone in need (1 John 3:17).

It's good to ask ourselves this question. "When was the last time I showed kindness to someone?" In Philippians 1:21 Paul says, *"For to me, to live is Christ and to die is gain."*

God's goal for us is the death of self-preservation – dying daily to our own desires and plans, and totally living for Christ.

7. Is Christ living in me?

Galatians 2:20: *I have been crucified with Christ; and it is no longer I who live, but Christ lives in me; and the life which I now live in the flesh I live by faith in the Son of God, who loved me and gave Himself up for me.*

If self effort could change us, we wouldn't need Jesus to do it for us. But we can't transform ourselves. It is Christ in us, the hope of glory. He is the source of our identity, our significance, and our strength.

Death to self is the only way to real life in Christ. Death before life! Death before power! Death before fruit! Less of us, and more of Him (John 3:30). The less there is of us, the more of the fruit of the Holy Spirit there will be in our lives.

John 12:23-25: *Jesus answered them, saying, "The hour has come for the Son of Man to be glorified. Truly, truly, I say to you, unless a grain of wheat falls into the earth and dies, it remains alone; but if it dies, it bears much fruit. He who loves his life loses it, and he who hates his life in this world will keep it to life eternal.*

If Jesus Christ lives in us, other people will see Him in us, and it will affect their lives for good and for God. Then, as we demonstrate confidence and faith in others, and believe in them, in what God has placed within them, they will be encouraged, built up, and become confident. This will give them motivation to go forward with God and spiritual growth to fulfil their destiny (Philippians 1:3-6).

People know if we really care for them and respect them. This will lead them to respond to God and to us. This kind of real kindness and care, and showing faith in someone, can make all the difference to their walk with God and their future destiny.

A Prayer

Help me, Lord Jesus, to be kind with Your kindness – and go the extra mile. Help me not to underestimate kindness in my life.

Help me to die to self daily, and live for You. Strengthen kindness in my life. Help me to be kind to my enemies, and to be an example of Your lovingkindness.

In Jesus' Name. Amen.

11. Seven Truths about Wisdom

From this Chapter

Wisdom is a gift from God. It is something we need to receive so that we can walk in wisdom, seeing what is right and what is wrong. God will anoint us with wisdom, and He sometimes gives us a word of wisdom for someone needing guidance and clarity in a particular situation. Wisdom is for the glory of God, and to do others good and bless them. Wisdom brings insight, discernment, and discretion. Then we can act wisely with others, and see the fruit of that (Proverbs 11:30).

1. We need Godly wisdom

James 3:17: *But the wisdom from above is first pure, then peaceable, gentle, reasonable, full of mercy and good fruits, unwavering, without hypocrisy.*

There is great wisdom in keeping God's law. True wisdom is much more than the wisdom of man. It is Godly wisdom. Godly wisdom is the greatest wisdom – having a great love and passion for God's Word and for God Himself.

The Word of God tells us to ask for more wisdom if we need it! (James 1:5). Trying to keep God's laws does not automatically mean we will go to Heaven. We must live in God's strength, not in our own. We need to admit we are sinners, and we need to say sorry for anything we have done wrong, and ask Jesus into our hearts and lives.

Jesus says He is the *only* way to Heaven. Jesus is the Saviour of the whole world, but we need to ask Him into our lives, and believe that He died on the cross for us to rescue us from the penalty of our sin – eternal death, separated from God.

Jesus is the way to bring us back to God. The only way. He paid the price for all sin for all time, and we can live the way He wants us to live – through His Holy Spirit living in us. And He gives us the power to do it!

2 Corinthians 5:21: *He made Him who knew no sin to be sin on our behalf, so that we might become the righteousness of God in Him.*

2. Walk wisely

Ephesians 5:15-17: *Therefore be careful how you walk, not as unwise men but as wise, making the most of your time, because the days are evil. So then do not be foolish, but understand what the will of the Lord is.*

There are times when we all need correction, help, and guidance from someone with more experience (Proverbs 19:20).

Wisdom is a gift from God. It is something we need to receive so that we can walk in wisdom, seeing what is right and what is wrong. God will anoint us with wisdom, and He sometimes gives us a word of wisdom for someone needing guidance and clarity in a particular situation.

Wisdom is for the glory of God, and to do others good and bless them. Wisdom brings insight, discernment, and discretion. Then we can act wisely with others, and see the fruit of that

(Proverbs 11:30).

Wisdom helps us in our day-to-day walk with God. We need to pray for wisdom for ourselves and for others (Colossians 1:9-10).

The wisest thing is always to submit to God's plan in our lives, even if it makes no sense to us. We simply need to be obedient. We need to walk in the light. (1 John 2:6).

3. Personal growth

Proverbs 3:18: *She is a tree of life to those who take hold of her, And happy are all who hold her fast.*

We have to be willing to pay the price for growth. If we don't grow, we stagnate. Spiritual growth is not automatic. It doesn't just happen. We need to take our own responsibility for growth. We need to be willing for change.

The Lord appeared to Solomon in the dream, and said to him, *"Ask what you wish Me to give you."* (1 Kings 3).

Solomon replied, *"Give Your servant an understanding heart to judge Your people to discern between good and evil. For who is able to judge this great people of Yours?"*

God was pleased with his request, so He also offered him both riches and honour as well! Wisdom and discernment made Solomon one of the greatest kings who ever reigned! 1 Kings 4:29: *Now God gave Solomon wisdom and very great discernment and breadth of mind, like the sand that is on the seashore.*

But, and here's a big warning, towards the end of his life Solomon forgot God and His ways, and brought disaster on his people. 1 Corinthians 10:12: *Therefore let him who thinks he stands take heed that he does not fall.*

4. Listen to God

Matthew 7:24-25: *"Therefore everyone who hears these words of Mine and acts on them, may be compared to a wise man who built his house on the rock. And the rain fell, and the floods came, and the winds blew and slammed against that house; and yet it did not fall, for it had been founded on the rock."*

Listen to His instructions and obey them. This is vital as we walk with our Heavenly Father. Jesus is our prime example. His main mission was to please His Father.

In verse 22 of this chapter we can see that we can talk Godly talk, refer to Him as Lord, and tell others about Him. We can cast out demons and do miracles, but the question that everything else and the hangs on is: *Do we obey our Father in Heaven?* We are not known by our gifts, but by the fruit of our character.

In verse 20 of the same chapter we see that a tree is identified by its fruit. A good tree cannot bring forth rotten fruit, and neither can a rotten tree bring forth good fruit. So we need to be wise and listen to God, and obey Him. We need to build on the solid foundation, just like the man who built his house on a rock.

5. Know what to take on

John 17:4: Jesus prayed, *"I glorified You on the earth, having accomplished the work which You have given Me to do."*

Jesus only did what His Father told Him to do. His desire was to please His Father, not Himself (John 5:19-20, 30). Some of the good things that come our way are not necessarily God's will for us. We need wisdom and discernment to know the difference.

If we spend a lot of our time with things that are not God's purpose for us, then we are in danger of becoming drained and burnt out. The things that seem good may keep us from the best that God has got for us.

We must only take things on if we have a peace that God is giving them to us. It's good to seek Him and listen to what He is saying to us, rather than just take things on face value. God knows our hearts, and if our heart is right in something, God will work on it with us and lead us the right way. He always wants the best for us!

Whatever God gives us to do, we must be aware that we need to rely on His strength, not on our own self effort which never works. It's God working through us.

God created us, and He has given us everything we need to do what He has called us to do. He has given us His power, His wisdom, and everything else that we need. We need to put our treasure, our talents and time, into God's Kingdom for His glory!

6. Know who to listen to

Proverbs 2:6: *For the Lord gives wisdom; From His mouth come knowledge and understanding.*

Is the company we are keeping encouraging wisdom and faith? Or is it increasing self-doubt? We must guard against someone else's limited thinking from hurting us. Negative thinking and talking can be very infectious. We need to keep focused on the greatness of our God. The Lord gives us wisdom to stay positive in our thinking and talking.

There may be people who don't encourage us in our potential and our calling. We *all* need encouragement! We need to listen to wisdom, knowledge and understanding, and be encouragers. Don't trust our own feelings. They can lead us the wrong way. The more we discipline ourselves to put the truth and wisdom of the Word of God first, the easier it will be to defeat the enemy.

We need to make a definite decision to focus on the right things, and follow them through (Colossians 3:2). Right focus gives us energy and power. It gives us motivation for the right things. Our mind will focus on the vision and the goal – a vision that God gives us. To be focused and persevere, we need to cut out distractions as Paul did and *"press on toward the goal for the prize of the upward call of God in Christ Jesus"* (Philippians 3:14).

We are running a race, and runners keep their eyes ahead, determined to reach their goal!

7. Keep learning!

Proverbs 15:14: *The mind of the intelligent seeks knowledge, But the mouth of fools feeds on folly.*

Learning and being willing to go on learning, and being stretched by God, is a great way to stay disciplined. We don't really forget what we learn. It's surprising the information that comes back to us years later. Learning can sometimes seem slow, but it's worth the time put into it.

If we are wise, we have a hunger to learn more, and to grow

and extend our borders. It is so important for us to remain teachable, whatever stage of life we are at.

Proverbs 9:9-11: *Give instruction to a wise man and he will be still wiser, Teach a righteous man and he will increase his learning. The fear of the Lord is the beginning of wisdom, And the knowledge of the Holy One is understanding. For by me your days will be multiplied, And years of life will be added to you.*

It's always good to learn more about the Word of God, so we can know God more, and grow in wisdom and faith. In 2 Timothy 3:16 Paul tells us that *all Scripture is inspired by God and profitable for teaching, for reproof, for correction, for training in righteousness.* It is a Living Word. It becomes active within us as we read and study it. As we look into its mirror, we see a reflection of where we are. This should cause us to act on it. The Word of God has power to cleanse, heal, deliver, and restore.

A prayer

Help me, Lord, to be wise in Your Godly wisdom. Help me to walk wisely, and to submit to Your plan for my life that I may grow in grace and faith, and listen to You.

Help me to please You in all that I do. Give me a hunger to learn and know You more.

In Jesus' Name. Amen.

12. Seven Truths about Holiness

From this Chapter

God wants all of our hearts. He wants us to be set apart for Him. It's a personal relationship that should affect every area of our lives. We no longer belong to ourselves, we belong to *Him*. He is our Father, and we are His children. We need to respond to the Holy Spirit's promptings when He wants us to let things go. It is always for our good. It will enhance our relationship with God, and bring us into greater freedom...

1. Christ in us!

1 Peter 1:15-16: *"Like the Holy One who called you, be holy yourselves also in all your behavior; because it is written, "You shall be holy, for I am holy."*

We are born again when we confess our sin and ask Jesus into our hearts. We then become part of God's family. God is holy, and we become holy – Christ in us! God's holiness is unique. He cannot be compared to anyone else (1 Samuel 2:2). There is no one like Him (Exodus 15:11).

Only God is holy and unchanging. God's presence turns ordinary ground into holy ground. God tells Moses in Exodus 3:1-6, to take off his shoes. Moses does as he's told, and covers his face. He's afraid to look at God.

Our relationship with God begins with Jesus in salvation – putting our faith in the sacrifice of Jesus on the cross for us. John: 1:29: *The next day he* [John the Baptist] *saw Jesus coming to him and said, "Behold, the Lamb of God who takes away the sin of the world!"* We have to accept Him as our Saviour who takes away our sin. Jesus then comes into our hearts and transforms our lives.

The presence of a Holy God in our hearts makes us holy (1 Peter 2:5). Through our relationship with God, and because of the blood of Christ, we are raised up together to sit with Him (Ephesians 2:4-7). *And* we are clothed with His righteousness!

2. Separated to God

Deuteronomy 6:5: *"You shall love the Lord your God with all your heart and with all your soul and with all your might."*

God wants all of our hearts. He wants us to be set apart for Him. It's a personal relationship that should affect every area of our lives. We no longer belong to ourselves, we belong to *Him.* He is our Father, and we are His children.

We need to glorify God in everything we do, and in everything we are. We must stop living the way we did before we were born again (1 Peter 1:14). Holiness is not something we can take or leave when it suits us. Holiness can't be compromised.

We need to be closely connected to Jesus and separated from the world. Separated from things that seem right, but aren't. We need to know the difference between good and evil, staying away from all that God says is unclean, impure, and morally wrong. We are *in* the world, but not *of* the world.

3. The Temple of the Holy Spirit

1 Corinthians 6:19-20: *Do you not know that your body is a temple of the Holy Spirit who is in you, whom you have from God, and that you are not your own? For you have been bought with a price: therefore glorify God in your body.*

The Holy Spirit lives in us! Our bodies are the Temple of the Holy Spirit. We need to listen to Him when He convicts us about anything wrong in our lives. There may be some sin that we hold onto. Or perhaps something that isn't sin, but it's not God's best for us. Something that we can do without.

Letting these things go will strengthen our walk with God, and make it richer. The things that defile us are wrong things that come from our hearts. Wrong thoughts, wrong attitudes, wrong actions and so on.

Acts 24:16: *In view of this, I also do my best to maintain always a blameless conscience both before God and before men.*

We need to respond to the Holy Spirit's promptings when He wants us to let things go. It is always for our good. It will enhance our relationship with God, and bring us into greater freedom, and anointing, and fruitfulness. It's best not to argue with God!

It is easy to miss the blessing of the richness of God's presence in our lives. When that happens, the enemy will rob us and use it to bring us into depression and despair. So we always need to be obedient to the Holy Spirit. It's never a good idea to rely on what seems right in our own eyes (Judges 17:6 and Proverbs 14:12).

Holiness is being wholly His! In every way! (Galatians 5:16-18).

4. Obedience to God's Word

1 John 1:5-7: *This is the message we have heard from Him and announce to you, that God is Light, and in Him there is no darkness at all. If we say that we have fellowship with Him and yet walk in the darkness, we lie and do not practice the truth; but if we walk in the Light as He Himself is in the Light, we have fellowship with one another, and the blood of Jesus His Son*

cleanses us from all sin.

We need to walk in the light of God's Word. His Word is Truth, our protection and guidance for life. If something doesn't agree with God's Word, leave it alone. It's no good for us. God never goes against His own Word. He will never lead us to do anything that His Word does not agree with.

Our thoughts, our actions, and our words should all agree with God's Word. We must be careful to follow the instructions in God's Word, and be expectant in faith. God's Word is a mirror. As we look into it, we see ourselves as we really are. We need to act on what we see – not just walk away and forget.

God's Word transforms our lives as we act upon it in faith, believing. It also protects and renews our minds (Romans 12:2).

There is mighty power in the Word of God – to heal, to save, to deliver, to transform, and to restore. There is nothing that God's Word cannot deal with.

2 Timothy 2:19: *Nevertheless, the firm foundation of God stands, having this seal, "The Lord knows those who are His," and, "Everyone who names the name of the Lord is to abstain from wickedness."*

5. Flee from sin and run to God

Psalm 32:3-6: *When I kept silent about my sin, my body wasted away Through my groaning all day long. For day and night Your hand was heavy upon me; My vitality was drained away as with the fever heat of summer. Selah. I acknowledged my sin to You, And my iniquity I did not hide; I said, "I will confess my transgressions to the Lord"; And You forgave the guilt of my sin. Therefore, let everyone who is godly pray to You in a time when You may be found; Surely in a flood of great waters they will not reach him.*

Sin in our lives gives the enemy too much scope. As soon as we are aware of sin, we need to repent and go in the opposite direction. Keep short accounts with God, so the enemy has no access point.

Sin deceives us and takes us in the wrong direction. Sin in our lives makes us fair game for the enemy. The Word of God says we can't serve two masters. God sees our hearts and the intentions of our hearts. The Holy Spirit will help us when we are willing to let go of the sin we cherish. Whatever we hang onto, will control us. As we let go, the control and bondage are broken.

As a redeemed child of God, when we sin wilfully and don't repent, we lose our peace and joy which is our strength. Repentance is extremely powerful. God doesn't leave us to live in our own strength. It's His Power in us that helps us to live the way He wants us to live. It's *His* power that changes us (Ephesians 1:19-21). We need to be filled with the Holy Spirit.

6. The whole Law fulfilled

Galatians 5:14-15: *For the whole Law is fulfilled in one word, in the statement, "You shall love your neighbor as yourself." But if you bite and devour one another, take care that you are not consumed by one another.*

As we love others, as we love ourselves, we fulfil the whole Law. We need to love and desire to keep God's Laws, and not harm one another with thoughtless words, or gossip. Holiness is single-minded focus. A pure desire for God's glory. Holiness is doing God's will each day with a desire to do what is right, no matter what the cost. It is separation from ungodly practices, from the ways of the world. Those who claim to follow Jesus Christ should believe and live according to God's Law.

John 17:15-16: Jesus prayed, *"I do not ask You to take them out of the world, but to keep them from the evil one. They are not of the world, even as I am not of the world."*

We are set apart for His use. We need to renounce the hidden things of darkness, and embrace God's Truth and His ways. Love is powerful. God is love, and we need to live in love.

1 John 4:8: *The one who does not love does not know God, for God is love.*

Love is absolutely essential to living in holiness. Love is a decision and choice. It's a matter of the will. Real love is not dependent on feelings. Feelings are important, but God's love will come through however we feel. When we put God's love into action, our feelings begin to line up with it!

7. We belong to His Kingdom

Colossians 1:13: *For He rescued us from the domain of darkness, and transferred us to the kingdom of His beloved Son.*

We need to remember that we are the expression of the Kingdom of God on Earth. We need to honour God, desiring to please Him. We need to honour our parents, respect and love them (Luke 2:51).

We need to serve others in love, to help the poor, having compassion, to live right lives – and keep away from anything grey or shady, and avoid any appearance of evil (1 Thessalonians 5:22). We must keep away from any occult involvement, and wherever we are or whatever we are doing we must watch our actions.

We are examples of God's Kingdom. We mustn't follow patterns of worldly behaviour. We must be careful what we listen to, and watch what we watch! We must be alert how we represent God's Kingdom, becoming more like Jesus every day.

We are Living Letters, read by everyone (2 Corinthians 3:2), bringing glory to God and His Kingdom. Let's display honesty, justice, and kindness, integrity and love.

Gideon told his army to watch him and follow him, and do what he did (Judges 7:17). It's good to ask ourselves what influence that would have on the people we know. Would it be helpful? Or would it be harmful for them? How would our example affect their lives?

We need to refuse to compromise, and live by the courage of our convictions. We need to walk the walk and talk the talk. Our words need to be in agreement with our character, with our behaviour, and with our love for others.

1 Peter 1:15-16: *Like the Holy One who called you, be holy yourselves also in all your behavior; because it is written, "You shall be holy, for I am holy."*

A Prayer

Help me, Lord Jesus, to give You all of my heart and my life, to be set apart for You. Help me to remember that I am the Temple of Your Holy Spirit. Help me to let go of the things that I need to let go of, so I can have Your best.

Help me to keep short accounts with You, and walk in the Light. Help me to love others the way You want me to.

In Jesus' Name. Amen.

Were the whole realm of nature mine
That were in offering far too small;
Love so amazing, so divine,
Demands my soul, my life, my all.

When I Survey the Wondrous Cross
Isaac Watts 1674–1748

13. Seven Truths about Accusation

From this Chapter

Satan reminds us of the sin and guilt of the past. He reminds us of all our wrongdoing, of all the things that have been forgiven by God. He loves to drag things up from the past to make us feel that we will never make it. We have to leave the guilt of the past behind. If we are born again, we are forgiven and set free from the guilt of the past. Once we have repented, we can move forward because God has cleared our record. In Christ we have become the righteousness of God. It may seem obvious, but if we don't leave the past behind, we can't go forward into the future. God does not accuse us. He wants to lift us up!

1.God does not accuse us

Zechariah 3:1-4: *Then he showed me Joshua the high priest standing before the angel of the Lord, and Satan standing at his right hand to accuse him. The Lord said to Satan, "The Lord rebuke you, Satan! Indeed, the Lord who has chosen Jerusalem rebuke you! Is this not a brand plucked from the fire?" Now Joshua was clothed with filthy garments and standing before the angel. He spoke and said to those who were standing before him, saying, "Remove the filthy garments from him." Again he said to him, "See, I have taken your iniquity away from you and will clothe you with festal robes."*

Zechariah's vision gives us a slight insight into the spirit world. As Joshua stands before the Lord, Satan is there too, accusing him. Seeing Satan resisting Joshua, is like seeing Satan resisting all of Israel, in effect. Satan always wants to stop anything of God being fulfilled.

When the Lord rebukes Satan, it is His response to Satan's accusations of Joshua. Satan loves to accuse God's people, but the Lord's rebuke stops the evil power in its tracks! We are God's *chosen* people. Satan *cannot* stop God's purposes.

Matthew 16:18-19: *I also say to you that you are Peter, and upon this rock I will build My church; and the gates of Hades will not overpower it. I will give you the keys of the kingdom of heaven; and whatever you bind on earth shall have been bound in heaven, and whatever you loose on earth shall have been loosed in heaven."*

Jesus comes to our defence before the Father, and reminds Him that the price of our sin has been paid in full! (Isaiah 53:7-9). Just as Joshua was clothed in new robes, so we are clothed in His righteousness. Totally justified. Account paid in full. Our God is a merciful God. If we feel accused and put down, it is Satan's work.

The Holy Spirit convicts us of sin, and shows us clearly what we need to do. Satan includes everything and makes us feel there is no way forward, that we have messed up and failed, that there is no way back. His plan is to make us want to give up on ourselves. He wants us to believe God is disappointed with us, and has given up on us.

Satan is the Father of Lies, he is our accuser, trying to fill us with fear, but he has been thrown down. He puts negative thoughts in our minds that tell us we will never make it. He tells us that we are not good enough, that we'll never come up to God's standard. He wants us to despair and give up. *But we don't have to live in condemnation and low self-worth.*

2. God wants to lift us up!

Colossians 1:13-14: *For He rescued us from the domain of darkness, and transferred us to the kingdom of His beloved Son, in whom we have redemption, the forgiveness of sins.*

We will never come up to God's standards by our own effort, but that is not a reason to give up – it's a reason to rejoice! Why? Because it's all about what Jesus has already done for us on the cross. It's *His Power* in us!

God's plan is to take us forward with Him into greater things. We need to put on the breastplate of righteousness, and the whole armour of God (Ephesians 6:14-18).

We have to leave the guilt of the past behind. If we are born again, we are forgiven and set free from the guilt of the past. Once we have repented, we can move forward because God has cleared our record. In Christ we have become the righteousness of God. It may seem obvious, but if we don't leave the past behind, we can't go forward into the future.

The accuser has no authority over us as a child of God. He is defeated and under our feet (Revelation 12:10-11). We have victory in Christ! The Holy Spirit tells us that all the past is forgiven, never to be remembered anymore (1 John 1:7-9).

Satan reminds us of the sin and guilt of the past. He reminds us of all our wrongdoing, of all the things that have been forgiven by God. He loves to drag things up from the past to make us feel that we will never make it.

The conviction of the Holy Spirit is clear. God puts His finger on something for our good, so we know that if we put it right with God, then we are forgiven, cleansed, and set free. His dealings with us are always to do us good.

3. Satan's disguise

2 Corinthians 11:13-14: *For such men are false apostles, deceitful workers, disguising themselves as apostles of Christ. No wonder, for even Satan disguises himself as an angel of light*

Satan comes dressed up – otherwise he wouldn't be able to trap us or trip us up. He would be too obvious. He comes as an angel of light. He can make us feel that God has rejected us because we are not holy enough. That we are not worthy, or not making the grade.

Satan wants us to see God as a judge who can never be pleased or satisfied, so we always feel lacking. John 3:17: *For God did not send the Son into the world to judge the world, but that the world might be saved through Him.*

Our Heavenly Father always loves us and totally understands us. He tells us that we lack nothing, because we have everything we need in Him. He is kind, loving, and forgiving. And if we need it, he will give us a fresh start with Him. He totally accepts us, and loves us unconditionally.

God sees us in Jesus, washed in His blood, and clothed in His righteousness. We are made worthy not because of anything we have done, but because of what Jesus has done! We are adopted into God's family, and we can call Him Abba, Father.

We are loved, accepted, forgiven, and secure, adopted by a loving Heavenly Father (Romans 8:15). We must never underestimate the power of the cross of Jesus Christ against all the power, plans, and schemes of Satan. God is All-Powerful. Satan has limited power.

4. The Word of God

John 14:26: Jesus said, *"But the Helper, the Holy Spirit, whom the Father will send in My name, He will teach you all things, and bring to your remembrance all that I said to you."*

The Holy Spirit brings to our remembrance Scriptures that we need to help us at the right time. That is why it is important to get as much Scripture inside us as we can, daily. We see in Scripture that God remains faithful to His promises to us (1 John 1:9). He remains faithful even if we are not always faithful to Him when we are going through a hard time (1 John 3:18-20).

If we rely on Jesus, there is no law that is effective against us. We are not under the law, but under grace. This is not to say that we can live any way we like. It is a relationship of love and grace, and if we love Him we want to please Him. We are not saved by keeping the law, but by our faith in Jesus. By grace, through faith, it is the gift of God. Ephesians 2:8-9: *For by grace you have been saved through faith; and that not of yourselves, it is the gift of God; not as a result of works, so that no one may boast.*

Be warned, Satan knows how to use Scripture to accuse us. He puts thoughts into our minds to try to make us feel that God's grace has been taken from us because we failed in doing our part in keeping the conditions. But remember, God's grace and love are unconditional! (Romans 10:3-4 and Galatians 2:16).

It is really important to know the Word of God, so we are not ignorant of Satan's devices. It is knowing the truth that sets us free (John 8:32).

5. Our feelings cannot be relied upon

Proverbs 3:5-6: *Trust in the Lord with all your heart and do not lean on your own understanding. In all your ways acknowledge Him, and He will make your paths straight.*

Satan will tell us that the way we feel is the truth. If we *feel* guilty, then we *are* guilty. Feelings like this are unfortunately very common. If we *feel* condemned, we feel we *are* condemned. But the Word of God tells us the truth.

Quite often our feelings don't agree with the Word of God, so they can lead us astray. "I *felt* it was right, or it *seemed* to be the right way to go." No, we cannot base our walk with God on our *feelings* – we must base it on the Word of God.

The Word of God tells us there is no condemnation (Romans 8:1-4 and Psalm 32:5). Our feelings will come into line with the Word of God if we trust the Word of God first, rather than trust how we feel.

Satan plays on our feelings, and he knows what negative and accusing thoughts to fill our minds with, in order to make us feel negative and guilty. What we think is what we will feel. And if we don't check it, we will eventually be drawn into negative action. Our feelings can be very strong, but also very wrong! So we need to focus and think on the right things which will bring our feelings into line with the Word of God.

Satan is a deceiver and a liar. He pretends to be what he is not. He comes in all sorts of disguises. He is the master of disguise.

Everything that God does, Satan counterfeits. Wherever there is something that is real there is always a copy, a counterfeit. When I worked with a team helping the homeless on the streets, one night we had a confrontation. The person said angrily, "You are just do-gooders. I bet you speak in tongues too! So do I."

At that point he spoke out loudly in tongues in his own voice. Then in a different voice he said, "You're not speaking to Him now, you fool. You are going to end up in hell like everyone else."

At that point we said, "You have come too late. We are covered in the blood of Jesus!"

He stood back and winced, and ran off shouting, "Help, help!"

No evil can stand in the presence and power of the blood of Jesus.

6. Satan wants to isolate us

Hebrews 10:23-25: *Let us hold fast the confession of our hope without wavering, for He who promised is faithful; and let us consider how to stimulate one another to love and good deeds, not forsaking our own assembling together, as is the habit of some, but encouraging one another; and all the more as you see the day drawing near.*

When Satan sows negative thoughts into our minds, he always has a plan that is destructive. He knows that certain suggestions he puts into our minds will cause us to want to withdraw from others. Accusations that make us feel unworthy, not acceptable, less significant than others. He can make us feel fearful of failure and defeat, so we feel inadequate when we are with others, especially if they seem to be stronger than we are in their faith. So we withdraw, and feel rejected by others. But all the time these feelings are based on Satan's lies about ourselves, making us feel lonely, hurt, unworthy, confused, and angry.

This is why it is so important to know the truth about ourselves as God sees us. We need to *believe* the truth of who we are in Christ, of how God sees us and loves us, and totally accepts us. Satan can be so convincing, especially when he plays on our weaknesses – which he does constantly. We need to be aware of our enemy, and stand strong in the Lord in the battle.

We need to wear our armour (Ephesians 6). We need to pray and read God's Word daily, to focus on the right things, and fill our minds with the Word of God. We need to stand in faith on the truth. And when we do, it's easier to spot the lies. We need to stay in fellowship with other believers. We need each other in the body of Christ.

7. It is not of God

2 Corinthians 10:4-5: *For the weapons of our warfare are not of the flesh, but divinely powerful for the destruction of fortresses. We are destroying speculations and every lofty thing raised up against the knowledge of God, and we are taking every thought captive to the obedience of Christ.*

If something disturbs us, gives us bad dreams, takes our peace, confuses us, puts guilt on us, discourages us, robs us of our joy – it is *not* from God!

Satan will try to convince us that we have no power, no calling, and no potential. He will remind us of all our disappointments. He will make us doubt ourselves and give us low self-worth so we feel it's hard to believe God for anything good, or anything new in our lives.

What we sow we reap. If we sow the Word of God, and prayer, and focus on the right things, and have regular fellowship, we will reap a godly life that is a testimony for Jesus Christ.

Today, we are showing the results of the things we sowed into our lives and meditated on yesterday. What we take in, will flow out to others.

Don't give lies, accusations and so on, room to grow. Don't allow them to hang around and take root, otherwise our minds will be vulnerable all the time to Satan's input.

We must let God have control of our minds. Satan tries to convince us that God is not big enough to forgive our sin, that unless we do everything just right, we are in trouble. That's a lie. When we fear failure, we limit ourselves.

God gives us freedom to fail! It's not about our performance being perfect. That's legalism. We must not let Satan have our day, our moods, or our thoughts.

We need to use our weapons of prayer, praise, the Word of God, and faith. God wants us to be full of life and growth. He is a great God, and He has so much more for us. He is a God of blessing and increase (James 4:7).

A prayer

Help me, Lord Jesus, to fill my mind with the right things. Make me aware of the difference between what is from You, and what comes from Satan. Give me discernment to know.

Help me to leave the past behind. Help me to keep things right with You, and remind me to use the weapons You have given me.

In Jesus' Name. Amen.

14. Seven Truths about Preparation

In this Chapter

We need to *get* prepared and then *stay* prepared. It's a lifetime of seeing the importance of being ready and prepared for the Master's use. Every day is a day that God has given us, a day that He has made. Let us use our time wisely and to the full, making each day count in the Kingdom of God as we come into alignment with His will and purposes for us.

We need to be living in a prepared state of readiness, always on our guard, ready with the Word of God, ready to use our gifts and talents at any time. We need to keep ourselves prepared, staying in tune and alignment with the Holy Spirit, keeping our house "clean" – *every* room, not just some, knowing who we are in Christ.

1. Preparation causes us to readjust

Ephesians 2:10: *For we are His workmanship, created in Christ Jesus for good works, which God prepared beforehand so that we would walk in them.*

When we are expectant for something to happen – we prepare. Preparation is high on God's list, and it should be high on ours! Preparation causes us to readjust our lives and our schedule. It also causes us to look forward, and see the importance of "today" to prepare for tomorrow.

Jesus had thirty years of preparation for three years of amazing ministry, fulfilling His destiny that changed history for ever. Joseph was in preparation for becoming Prime Minister of Egypt for many years of his life (Genesis 41:41).

Noah prepared for the flood. He was expectant, he was obedient. He built the Ark on dry ground! He believed and trusted God, and obeyed Him totally (Genesis 6:22).

Noah activated his faith *before* the rains and the flood came. It didn't look as though it was going to happen, but Noah believed God against all the odds. So he was prepared. God prepares us. Part of God's preparation in our lives is to do with our own response to His instruction in the unknown, in challenging times. Through these things God refines us, increases our faith, stretches us, and develops us. He prepares us for what He has planned for us ahead.

Although God is preparing us, we need to do our part in being prepared, always being aware that God is working in us constantly. We need to come into alignment with His Word, and do our part in responding from our hearts to Him (Ezekiel 38:7).

2. **God uses prepared people!**

1 Kings 18:41-45: *Now Elijah said to Ahab, "Go up, eat and drink; for there is the sound of the roar of a heavy shower." So Ahab went up to eat and drink. But Elijah went up to the top of Carmel; and he crouched down on the earth and put his face between his knees. He said to his servant, "Go up now, look toward the sea."*

So he went up and looked and said, "There is nothing."

And he said, "Go back" seven times.

It came about at the seventh time, that he said, "Behold, a cloud as small as a man's hand is coming up from the sea."

And he said, "Go up, say to Ahab, 'Prepare your chariot and go down, so that the heavy shower does not stop you.'"

In a little while the sky grew black with clouds and wind, and there was a heavy shower. And Ahab rode and went to Jezreel.

Elijah was single-minded and expectant and prepared. He believed against the odds, and he didn't give up. He sent his servant out to look seven times to see if rain was coming. He was convinced it would come, and he saw the rainstorm with the eye of faith.

Whatever we are called to do, it's good to live in preparation so we are ready any time God wants to use us, and move through us by His Spirit for others and for His Kingdom.

We need to *get* prepared and then *stay* prepared. It's a lifetime of seeing the importance of being ready and prepared for the Master's use. Preparation very much hinges on what we believe. We see "today" in a different way when we believe that tomorrow's fruitfulness and effectiveness depend on our preparation today. The Word of God tells us to be wise and number our days (Psalm 90:12).

Every day is a day that God has given us, a day that He has made. Let us use our time wisely and to the full, making each day count in the Kingdom of God as we come into alignment with His will and purposes for us. Our days and our lives affect many other lives – either positively or negatively.

3. We need to clean house

2 Chronicles 29:5: *Then he said to them, "Listen to me, O Levites. Consecrate yourselves now, and consecrate the house of the Lord, the God of your fathers, and carry the uncleanness out from the holy place."*

If we want to grow spiritually and go to new levels with God, we need to reflect regularly on where we are with God, what we are doing for Him and why. We need to be constantly checking motives and asking what God wants us to carry on doing, and what He wants us to finish with!

As in our natural houses, things can pile up over time. Maybe things that clutter, or things we don't use that need removing! So it is with our spiritual house. We need to allow God to clear out the clutter of the old season, to make space for the new things in the new season.

We can sometimes get foggy in our vision, and things can sometimes creep in unawares, and get out of perspective. When that happens, we need to get back on track, and into line with the Holy Spirit, and have clear vision again. With clear vision we can go forward with God. Sometimes we need to let go of the *good* things in order to get the *best*.

God always wants us to have His best, and remove those things that distance us from Him. This is all part of the process of preparing us for going to new levels with Him. God is always moving us on, and He wants to take us to greater things.

4. Being prepared for Christ's return

Philippians 3:20-21: *For our citizenship is in heaven, from which also we eagerly wait for a Saviour, the Lord Jesus Christ; who will transform the body of our humble state into conformity with the body of His glory, by the exertion of the power that He has even to subject all things to Himself.*

We need to be salt and light in the dark world. We need to shine in the darkness. People need to see the difference in us because of God's presence. His presence sets us apart. We are called to be a blessing, and we need to live in the preparation and expectancy of Jesus' return. We need to know that we are ready and prepared to meet with Him.

We need to be using our gifts, fulfilling our calling, having regular fellowship, and keeping our lives right. We need to spend quality time in prayer and reading the Word of God (Hebrews 10:24-25). We need to stay alert and on our toes! (Matthew 25:13).

No one knows the time of His return, but we have the assurance in the Word of God that He will come again. So we need t watch and pray, and make sure we are ready and prepared for His appearing. What a day that will be!

We need to be fulfilling what God has called us to do, to be using our talents and not burying them like the unprofitable servant (Matthew 25:25). What we use for God will grow and develop and increase, so we will hear the words, "Well done, good and faithful servant."

Are we putting His Kingdom first? Let us lay up our treasure in heaven, not in the things that will fade away. We need to be sure we have put our lives right with God by accepting Jesus into our hearts and lives. We will know our sins are forgiven as we say sorry to God. We will know we are going to Heaven when we leave this earth. The only way to Heaven is through Jesus! When Jesus returns, He will take us with Him if we belong to Him. If not, we will be left behind.

We need to be ready and prepared for Jesus' return. Let's be building and preparing for eternity. John 14:1-3: *"Do not let your heart be troubled; believe in God, believe also in Me. In My Father's house are many dwelling places; if it were not so, I would have told you; for I go to prepare a place for you. If I go and prepare a place for you, I will come again and receive you to Myself, that where I am, there you may be also."*

5. The prepared plan of Salvation

John 7:8: *"Go up to the feast yourselves; I do not go up to this feast because My time has not yet fully come."*

In the fullness of time Jesus died on the cross. This was God's prepared plan and purpose for all mankind. There was a perfect time for His birth and for His death. When Jesus was in Bethany a woman comes to the home of Simon the leper to anoint Him with some precious ointment – very costly perfume.

The disciples are indignant about it being a waste, because it was so expensive. Jesus comes to the woman's defence and tells them that she did it in preparation for His burial (Matthew 26:6-13 and Hebrews 10:5-7). His was a body prepared for the salvation of all mankind.

Jesus honoured the woman very highly (verse 13). Oh the

love that drew salvation's plan, Oh the grace that brought it down to man, Oh the mighty gulf that God did span – at Calvary!

Romans 5:6: *For while we were still helpless, at the right time Christ died for the ungodly.*

There is a prepared time for everything in God's amazing plan. What a sacrifice! What a gift! God, through His only Son, opens all of Heaven up to us! And what joys await us there – the joy of seeing our Saviour face-to-face!

6. A God of Plan, Purpose and Preparation

Proverbs 16:9: *The mind of man plans his way, but the Lord directs his steps.*

We have God's promise that He will direct us. We must not be afraid to make plans and prepare. He will direct our steps. He expects us to make plans and prepare, at the same time trusting Him completely to take us the right way. God sees our hearts, and if our heart is to do His will, then He will keep us on the right path (Isaiah 30:21).

God's love for us is fixed and eternal. He has a definite plan and purpose for each one of us. He is in control of our lives as we give them to Him, and allow Him to take the reins.

He always wants to give us good things, and sometimes the good things come from difficult situations that we go through. But in His purpose, God works all things for our good. When we go through hard times and attacks from Satan, God will bring a blessing from it as we recognise that *He* is in control, not Satan. Satan needed God's permission to attack Job (Job 2:6). God is the All Powerful One, not Satan (Matthew 28:18).

So, God is in control and is always working for us and in us to bring His plans and purposes to pass. He is always preparing us for the things He has for us in the future, and He will use the most unlikely things to do it! (1 John 4:4).

7. The preparation of the Gospel of Peace

Ephesians 6:15: ... *and having shod your feet with the preparation of the gospel of peace.*

Be strong in the Lord and in the strength of His might (verse

10). We must remember to wear our full armour, and be constant in prayer. Our struggle is not with flesh and blood (verse 12). Let's be prepared to share the gospel every chance we get, that we will be alert and awake to the needs of people around us – in our everyday lives hearing the voice of the Holy Spirit as He instructs us.

We need to be living in a prepared state of readiness, always on our guard, ready with the Word of God, ready to use our gifts and talents at any time. We need to keep ourselves prepared, staying in tune and alignment with the Holy Spirit, keeping our house "clean" – *every* room, not just some, knowing who we are in Christ (Isaiah 43:1).

It is important to see that we are not who *people* say we are, but who *God* says we are. We need to know who we are in God's eyes, to know how God sees us. We are complete in Jesus Christ. God sees us covered in the blood of Jesus, and clothed in His righteousness. In Jesus we are totally accepted and loved, adopted into God's family. Now we can call Him Abba, Father (2 Corinthians 5:21 and Colossians 2:10). It is in Jesus that we are made totally worthy!

1 Corinthians 2:9: *but just as it is written, "Things which eye has not seen and ear has not heard, And which have not entered the heart of man, All that God has prepared for those who love Him."*

A prayer if you already know Jesus

Help me, Lord, to have You at the centre of my life, to allow You to prepare me and to help me grow in You. Help me to live in preparation, ready for Your return and ready to be used by You at any time.

Help me to be wise with my time, to keep my life right before You, and to be obedient to You and Your Word. Strengthen my prayer life.

In Jesus' Name. Amen.

A prayer if you would like to ask Jesus into your life

Dear Lord Jesus, please forgive me for every sin in my life. I am sorry, and I ask for Your forgiveness.

Thank You, Jesus, for dying on the cross for me, to set me free from the penalty and grip of my sin. Please come into my heart, and fill me with Your Holy Spirit.

Thank You, Jesus. Amen.

15. Seven Truths about Kingdom Living

In this Chapter

"Your kingdom come, Your will be done, On earth as it is in heaven." Is that our passion? The world says, "The more I grab hold of and keep, the richer I get!" The Kingdom of God says, "The more I give away, the more I receive!" We are the expression of the Kingdom of God in the earth – His love, His power, His healing, His peace, His deliverance, His presence and His abundant life!

We need to enter into the truth of who we are, and what we have in Jesus – and live in the power of it. We have been given power and authority in Jesus' Name over all the power of the enemy. We have His Resurrection Power living in us!

1. Seek first the Kingdom

Matthew 6:33: *But seek first His kingdom and His righteousness, and all these things will be added to you.*

In 2 Chronicles 1:7-12 God appears to Solomon, and tells him, "Ask what I shall give you." King Solomon shows his gratitude to God for His goodness to his father David, and for making him king, and he asks for wisdom and knowledge to rule the people well.

God is pleased with Solomon's reply, because he hasn't asked for personal wealth and honour, or long life. So God gives him wisdom and knowledge. But God also gives him what he didn't ask for – riches, wealth and honour, such as no other king has had before him or will do after him.

Solomon's desire was to help his people, with *God's* help. God commended him highly, and blessed him beyond expectation. God gave him above and beyond what he had asked for!

The more we are ready to die to ourselves and what we want, the more God will bless us. The more we give, the more we receive.

"Your kingdom come, Your will be done, On earth as it is in heaven." Is that our passion? King Solomon recognised he needed God's wisdom to give the people the best. The world says, "The more I grab hold of and keep, the richer I get!" The Kingdom of God says, "The more I give away, the more I receive!"

2. **All Jesus has – we have**

Romans 8:17: *and if children, heirs also, heirs of God and fellow heirs with Christ, if indeed we suffer with Him so that we may also be glorified with Him.*

The last part regarding the sufferings is easily forgotten or missed. We need to remember and be willing to be living sacrifices, all on the altar for Him. We have our inheritance in Him. We are kings and priests to our God.

1 Peter 2:9-10: *But you are a chosen race, a royal priesthood, a holy nation, a people for God's own possession, so that*

you may proclaim the excellencies of Him who has called you out of darkness into His marvelous light; for you once were not a people, but now you are the people of God; you had not received mercy, but now you have received mercy.

We need to receive the Word of God and His promises by faith, and activate them by putting our faith to work. And as we do, our faith will grow stronger. We already have everything we need for life and holiness in Jesus, through the power of the Holy Spirit.

1 John 4:16-17: *We have come to know and have believed the love which God has for us. God is love, and the one who abides in love abides in God, and God abides in him. By this, love is perfected with us, so that we may have confidence in the day of judgment; because as He is, so also are we in this world.*

We are the expression of the Kingdom of God in the earth – His love, His power, His healing, His peace, His deliverance, His presence and His abundant life! We need to enter into the truth of who we are, and what we have in Jesus – and live in the power of it. We have His Resurrection Power living in us!

We have been given power and authority in Jesus' Name over all the power of the enemy.

Luke 10:17-20: *The seventy returned with joy, saying, "Lord, even the demons are subject to us in Your name." And He said to them, "I was watching Satan fall from heaven like lightning. Behold, I have given you authority to tread on serpents and scorpions, and over all the power of the enemy, and nothing will injure you. Nevertheless do not rejoice in this, that the spirits are subject to you, but rejoice that your names are recorded in heaven."*

We are a temple. God's Spirit and His life dwell in us (1 Corinthians 3:16). We are joint heirs with Christ (Romans 8:17). We are secure in God's love (Romans 8:35-39).

The same Spirit that raised Jesus from the dead dwells in us (Romans 8:11).

3. Faith is the assurance of things hoped for

Hebrews 11:1: *Now faith is the assurance of things hoped for, the conviction of things not seen.* Jesus pointed out that we live in a faithless generation. Matthew 17:17: *And Jesus answered and said, "You unbelieving and perverted generation, how long shall I be with you? How long shall I put up with you? Bring him here to Me."*

This means that we will often come into contact with the negative attitudes of many people. Unless we recognise this, it can wear us down by weakening our faith. That is why we need to strengthen our faith daily in God's Word (Matthew 17:20)

Jesus is talking about using our faith today – now! And He also talks about having faith the size of a mustard seed. A mustard seed is very small – tiny – but it grows into a tree large enough for the birds to nest in its branches. We all have a measure of faith given to us by God. When we activate it – miracles happen!

We need to have an attitude of faith, and speak words of faith. It is then that faith works, and we see what is possible.

Radical faith stands strong, and is determined even if there are hard things going on at the moment. Faith will stand its ground and still believe and trust God. We need to feed our faith. Our faith sustains us.

As we read God's Word, and get it into us and get ourselves into it, we will experience more of the power of His Word in our lives. There will be an increase in faith, a renewing of our minds, a quenching of our thirst as God's Word feeds us with fresh bread everyday. Manna from heaven! God's Word will bring out our potential that God has put within us from before the beginning.

Mark 11:22-24: *And Jesus answered saying to them, "Have faith in God. Truly I say to you, whoever says to this mountain, 'Be taken up and cast into the sea,' and does not doubt in his heart, but believes that what he says is going to happen, it will be granted him. Therefore I say to you, all things for which you pray and ask, believe that you have received them, and they will be granted you."*

4. Whenever you stand praying, forgive

Mark 11:25-26: *Whenever you stand praying, forgive, if you have anything against anyone, so that your Father who is in heaven will also forgive you your transgressions. But if you do not forgive, neither will your Father who is in heaven forgive your transgressions."*

Unforgiveness is a big blockage to receiving anything from God. We need to live in forgiveness, and keep our hearts right.

If we do not forgive, we will not be forgiven. So forgive, and we set ourselves free. When we don't forgive ourselves, we lock ourselves into what we don't forgive. We live in the grip of it. God has given us the power to forgive and let go.

We can depend on what God says, and He will never tell us to do something that we *cannot* do. We need to know who we are in God's eyes, and grasp what we have in Him. If we don't know who we are in God, then Satan will play on making us feel unworthy, guilty and condemned.

God's grace and unconditional love for us is amazing. It is our only sure security to base our self-worth on. Knowing who we are, gives us confidence in ourselves, and in what God has placed within us. God sees us "in Christ," clothed in His righteousness, washed in His blood, and totally accepted and adopted into our Father's family.

This is *not* because of anything we have done, but because of what Jesus has done on the cross for us. He who knew no sin became sin for us, so we can be debt free, with a clean record. *And* He has raised this up together with Him to sit with Him in Heavenly Places (Ephesians 2:6). We are *richly* blessed!

5. Use the greatness that's within us

Ephesians 3:20-21: *Now to Him who is able to do far more abundantly beyond all that we ask or think, according to the power that works within us, to Him be the glory in the church and in Christ Jesus to all generations forever and ever. Amen.*

If we use what we have, others won't be cheated out of it. Use what we have, and the ripples go out far and wide.

Jesus calls us to leave all fear behind, to take risks in faith and obedience, and live in the fullness of who God made us to be. What do we need from Jesus? Press into Him, don't give up, be radical and relentless. We are sustained by purpose and persistence. It's the difference between those who fulfil the dream, and those who just dream! The just shall live by faith – it's a lifestyle of faith.

Whatever God's Word says about us, we need to say – and agree with! What God has placed in us will change what is on the outside of us. As we put it to work, what is within us is greater than anything we have been through in the past – anything we are going through now, or any obstacles that are in the way.

When things around us are saying Stop, and something inside us is saying Go, that is God working in us to make us willing and able to obey Him (Philippians 2:13).

6. He who abides in love abides in God

1 John 3:14: *We know that we have passed out of death into life, because we love the brethren. He who does not love abides in death.*

God is love! If we don't walk and live in love, then we are not abiding in God. Everything we do has to be done in love. Love is the fruit of the Holy Spirit that covers all (Proverbs 10:12). All that we are and do has to be motivated by love.

God has shown us the greatest love of all when He sent His only Son to die in our place. Such love!

It's not by our power, our gifts, our exploits, or our talent that we are known. It is by our love for each other. Love is not selfish or unkind. Love does not put ourselves first, but thinks of others first (1 Corinthians 13). We are told by Jesus not only to love the lovable, but to love our enemies, and also love those who we find hard to love (Matthew 5:44). His love has been poured out in our hearts through the Holy Spirit (Romans 5:5).

There is no fear in love (1 John 4:18). His perfect love casts out all fear.

Love is much more than a feeling. Jesus commands us to love one another. We should always choose to love. We are told to put on love (Colossians 3:14). We need to love in action, in truth, not just in words (1 John 3:18). As we do the right thing and reach out in love, our feelings will come into line with our actions. We just need to be willing, and make the right choice. Jesus never stops loving us! He knows us at our worst, and still loves us more than anyone else does.

What we have received we need to give away.

7. We need to embrace all that we have and all that we are in Jesus

Hebrews 12:28-29: *Therefore, since we receive a kingdom which cannot be shaken, let us show gratitude, by which we may offer to God an acceptable service with reverence and awe; for our God is a consuming fire.*

We are the army of God! God is preparing us, making us ready for what He has for us in the future. He works in us by His Holy Spirit. All the time, day and night, He changes us into all that He has purposed for us to be. And He is so patient with us!

We can rely on what God's Word says. It will always accomplish the purpose for which it is sent (Isaiah 55:11). By God's Word the earth and the heavens came into being (Psalm 33:9).

We need to speak God's Word. It is a powerful double-edged sword that pierces through the hardest situations. God's Word has great authority and power. The forces of darkness around us today have to submit to the power of God's Word (Luke 4:32-36). We need to read it often, and meditate on it, stand on it by faith, and speak it out (Colossians 3:16).

It is when the Word of God is given pre-eminence in our lives that it keeps us on the right track, and it helps us to receive revelation and insight, and become more aware of God's voice speaking to us. Paul found that embracing Jesus Christ and His purpose in his life was more important than anything (Philippians 3:7-8).

There was a time when Paul thought many other things were important, but he found out that his true identity was in his relationship with Jesus. That was where he was truly secure – not in anything he himself had accomplished.

Whatever we let go of we will get back many times over. With God's Kingdom, letting go is gain!

* What would you ask God for? One thing.

* Seek first the Kingdom.
* Less of us – more of Him.
* When we pray – forgive.
* We are the expression of the Kingdom of God in the earth.
* Embrace all that we are, and all that we have in Jesus.
* The more we let go – the more we gain.
* Activate our faith.
* Speak and agree with God's Word.
* Live in His love.

A Prayer

Help me, Lord Jesus, the put Your Kingdom first in my life. Let there be less of me and more of You. Help me to live in forgiveness. Show me how to be the expression of Your Kingdom in the earth.

Help me to embrace all that I have and all that I am in You, that I might freely give. Help me to activate my faith and live in Your love.

In Jesus' Name. Amen.

16. Seven Ways *Not* to be a Chameleon!

About this Chapter

The chameleon blends into its surroundings. Wherever it is, it does not need to stand out, because of its ability to camouflage itself. It can blend in anywhere. In our uniqueness, how can we blend in? We do not *need* to blend in. We need to *stand out* in the power that God has placed within us through His Holy Spirit. What has God empowered us and envisioned us for? Are we standing out – or are we trying to blend in? Are we letting our light shine, or are we hiding it?

1. Live in the power of our uniqueness

Matthew 19:26: *Looking at them Jesus said to them, "With people this is impossible, but with God all things are possible."*

Our faith is energised when we live in expectancy, thinking and believing in faith, and speaking words of truth and life in faith.

The tongue brings life – or death. Our minds need renewing daily. We need to speak, to think, and act in agreement with the Word of God. We need to see by faith beyond where we are right now.

If we have a goal and a vision, we need to act in faith as if we are already seeing it come to pass – like Abraham who counted the stars in the sky. He believed God against the odds. And they were great. And God's promise came to pass.

David won the victory over the giant because he moved in the power of his uniqueness. He was equipped in a unique way to conquer. Our identity is not in what we *do*. But, when we fulfil our vision, our calling, we move in the power of our uniqueness.

The chameleon blends into its surroundings. Wherever it is, it does not need to stand out, because of its ability to camouflage itself. It can blend in anywhere. It changes colour to suit its surroundings to fool its predators.

We were born to fulfil our vision, our destiny, *to stand out* in the power of what God has placed within us. We were *not* called to blend in and become complacent and hidden!

2. Have a dream and a goal

Acts 26:19: Paul said, *"So, King Agrippa, I did not prove disobedient to the heavenly vision,"*

We need to be willing to do our part in order to see the dream, which God has given us, come to pass. Twelve spies entered the Promise Land, but only two of the twelve who came back said they were well able to overcome it (Numbers 13:30). The others thought it was impossible!

When we have expectancy and faith for the future, we go forward into that future believing that anything is possible, because of the power of God at work within us.

Ephesians 3:20-21: *Now to Him who is able to do far more abundantly beyond all that we ask or think, according to the power that works within us, to Him be the glory in the church and in Christ Jesus to all generations forever and ever. Amen.*

Where are we focusing? On God? He is the only One who can bring it to pass. We need to have a goal that is beyond our ability and beyond our comfort zone. Growth will come with change. We must never settle for where we are spiritually, because there is always more.

We need to believe that there are greater things for us with God. No matter what comes against us, or tries to quench the fire of the Holy Spirit within us, we need to stand strong in the power of God's might, and see His purposes come to pass.

When our vision is born of God, it will benefit many people. Desire and destiny are linked. A desire that has become stronger, and stays with us, is usually a pointer to our destiny.

We need to water our vision and keep it alive, to speak life into it and activate it. We need to encourage ourselves in the Word of God. David strengthened himself in the Lord (1 Samuel 30:6). We need to build ourselves up in our faith (Jude 20). We need to challenge things, but love should always be the motivating force.

In our uniqueness, how can we blend in? We do not *need* to blend in, We need to *stand out* in the power that God has placed within us through His Holy Spirit.

3. Be who we are

Ephesians 1:11-12: *Also we have obtained an inheritance, having been predestined according to His purpose who works all things after the counsel of His will, to the end that we who were the first to hope in Christ would be to the praise of His glory.*

We have to be who God has made us to be, for the sake of others – wherever we are, and whoever we are with. God wants us to be free to be ourselves, not to hide who we really are in Him. It is the transforming power of the Holy Spirit in us that blesses others. If we hold back from being the unique person God wants us to be, we withhold from others something that God wants to give them.

We are most powerful when we are ourselves in God – when we share our love and our passion, our hunger for His Presence.

Sometimes we need to fall in love with Jesus all over again! (Revelation 2:4). We must not stifle or stunt what we have, and all that we are, in God.

Whatever atmosphere we are in, we need to show God's love and grace. That is when we will change the atmosphere around us by the Holy Spirit.

If we are aware of who we are and what we have in God, we will use our power and authority over all the powers of darkness (1 John 4:4). We are His masterpiece, the expression of the Kingdom of God on earth.

We are united with Christ and have an inheritance with Him. God loves us more than anything we will ever do for Him (Ephesians 2:4-5). Our greatest glory is that we belong to Him. We are His. We must be the unique person that God intends us to be, and tap into the power of that. Remember, we are very significant in the Kingdom of God.

4. Put down the fear of man

Proverbs 29:25: *The fear of man brings a snare, But he who trusts in the Lord will be exalted.*

If the approval of other people is greater to us than God's approval, we are in a prison of our own making and we will find it hard to feel secure.

Trusting God means safety and security in His approval. If we put ourselves at the mercy of the approval of other people, we will be influenced by their opinions and moods. Our true worth is only to be found in God. Fear of others brings insecurity. We are afraid to be ourselves in case we upset someone, or meet with their disapproval. It means always trying to please, never saying No.

In the Word of God Jesus said No many times (John 2:3-4). He said No to His mother when the wine ran out (Luke 4:3-4). He said No to the devil in the wilderness (Luke 5:16). Jesus said No to the demands of others, and he didn't apologise for it! We can end up in the trap of helping others, simply to meet a need in ourselves.

Real ministry to others comes through those who know they

are loved by God. This ministry is natural and easy. It comes from the overflow of a committed relationship with Jesus – otherwise we burn out (Matthew 11:29-30).

5. The disciples stood out!

Mark 8:27-29: *Jesus went out, along with His disciples, to the villages of Caesarea Philippi; and on the way He questioned His disciples, saying to them, "Who do people say that I am?" They told Him, saying, "John the Baptist; and others say Elijah; but others, one of the prophets." And He continued by questioning them, "But who do you say that I am?" Peter answered and said to Him, "You are the Christ."*

What has God empowered us and envisioned us for? Are we standing out – or are we trying to blend in? Are we letting our light shine, or are we hiding it? In these verses in Mark chapter 8, Peter recognises who Jesus Christ is. "You are the Christ!" What a revelation (Luke 10:17-20).

In these verses we read that the disciples returned with joy for what they were seeing. And Jesus reminds them to rejoice more that they are going to heaven.

The disciples' lives showed the power of Jesus! They made waves wherever they went. They stood out for truth and righteousness, for power and authority. Our lives will show what we mostly focus on.

An Anglican Bishop said, "Why is it that everywhere the apostle Paul went they had a revolution, but everywhere I go they have a cup of tea?"

Paul stood out!

1 Corinthians 15:58: *Therefore, my beloved brethren, be steadfast, immovable, always abounding in the work of the Lord, knowing that your toil is not in vain in the Lord.*

Matthew 6:33: *"But seek first His kingdom and His righteousness, and all these things will be added to you."*

We must ask ourselves is there anything holding us back? Something making us hide our talents and stop us being all that God is calling us to be? Knowing what is holding us back is what enables us to deal with it, and start moving forward. We all have gifts and talents to use in the plan of God (Romans 12:6-8).

We need to act on opportunities as they come, and trust God for what only He can do. Opportunities to use our gifts and our talents come in many different ways. Sometimes it will be a thought that God gives us, or through a word from someone else. Or a contact God brings our way, or something that grabs our attention.

It is always good to wait prayerfully before God, and then trust Him to direct our steps as we act on it. Unless we sense through the Holy Spirit leading us we have no peace about following it through. He will show us clearly the direction to take if we are willing.

Some prompting from the Holy Spirit can be missed at the time if we are not close enough to hear. This is why it is so important to live as close to God as we can, with time set aside for daily prayer and Bible reading.

6. No comparison

Romans 12:4-5: *For just as we have many members in one body and all the members do not have the same function, so we, who are many, are one body in Christ, and individually members one of another.*

We must not compare ourselves with others. If we think other Christians are better than us, then we feel inadequate and we underestimate what we have from God. And if we think others are worse than we are, we can get proud and puffed up. Whichever way – we lose!

We are many parts in the body of Christ, and we need each other for the body to work as it should. If our part is not functioning, then the whole body is affected. Each one of us is an important part, and the whole body suffers without our part. We must not see another person as being more important in the body of Christ than we are, because every part is significant in the functioning of the whole body together as one.

When we have jealousy or resentment at another's success, we will lose our joy and peace. And when we try to copy someone else, we lose out on what God has given us – something that is unique and powerful. Trying to be like someone else is like trying to blend in, especially if the other person seems to be more accepted than we are.

This whole feeling is based on a lie. The lie is that we are less important than others are. The truth is that we are just as significant to the body as we are to Jesus Christ who is the Head of the body. We are totally loved and accepted by Him, and a very important and necessary part of the whole body.

So there's no need to fear about stepping out and being *you*! Each one of us has something to give that no one else has, because each one of us is a designer original – a one-off. We need to believe in what God has placed within us – and use it!

7. Keep our priorities in place

Hebrews 2:1: *For this reason we must pay much closer attention to what we have heard, so that we do not drift away from it.*

Our greatest priority in life should be our relationship with Jesus, keeping Him in the centre of everything. We need to be obedient, doing His will, and thereby fulfilling our destiny. Then we will be all that He made us to be. It is our responsibility to keep our spiritual priorities in place. God won't do it for us. We pay a price if we let our priorities slip away. We lose out.

Are we listening to His voice? Are we spending time with Him? God is working in us all the time, so we can be ready for what He has for us next. Time spent with God is gain. Always gain.

We were made to glorify God, and enjoy His presence (1 Corinthians 10-31). So let us glorify God in everything we do, and with all we are. Hear Him, obey Him, and enjoy Him.

We can enjoy His presence when our lives are pleasing Him, and lived to glorify Him. We were made to be fruitful (John 15:16). The closer we are to God, the more fruitful we will be.

We must keep our priorities in balance, and put God first. We must not get distracted by being over-busy with so many things that we don't have time for the things that really matter (John 15:2).

God prunes us so that we can bear even more fruit. If we allow Him to, He cuts back the dead branches, and also cuts back living branches. This process causes more growth. He cuts the good as well, so we get the "best."

Sometimes we may wonder what is happening. God is pruning us for greater growth and fruitfulness.

As we submit to Him, He knows exactly what He's doing with us. It is always for our own good to let Him take us where He wants us to be with Him. He "prunes" us because He loves us too much to leave us exactly as we are!

A Prayer

Dear Lord Jesus, help me to live in the power of my uniqueness, to have a dream and a goal. Help me to be all that I am in You. Deliver me from the fear of other people. Help me not to hide my talents or try to be someone else. Help me to stand out in *Your* power, and not try to blend in. Help me to keep my priorities right with You.

In Jesus' Name. Amen.

17. Seven Ways to Change Your Perspective

From this Chapter

There are so many distractions around us today. Paul found that there was nothing more important than eternal things. Everything else will fade away and come to an end. If we are busy focusing on material and temporal things, we will have no time to focus on what really matters. If we want to see things from a different perspective, some of the greatest growth and changes will come through God's Word at work in us.

When we recognise who we are in Jesus, then our perspective will change in the way we see circumstances, in the way we see others, and in the way we see ourselves. We need to feel good about ourselves, about what God has placed within us.

1. Knowing what matters most

Philippians 3:7: *But whatever things were gain to me, those things I have counted as loss for the sake of Christ.*

There are so many distractions around us today. Paul found that there was nothing more important than eternal things. Everything else will fade away and come to an end. If we are busy focusing on material and temporal things, we will have no time to focus on what really matters.

Matthew 6:19-21: Jesus said, *"Do not store up for yourselves treasures on earth, where moth and rust destroy, and where thieves break in and steal. But store up for yourselves treasures in heaven, where neither moth nor rust destroys, and where thieves do not break in or steal; for where your treasure is, there your heart will be also."*

Paul was caught up in persecuting God's people. He imprisoned them, acting violently in his goal to pursue a religious vendetta against the early Christians.

But Paul knew God's grace in his life when he had an encounter with Jesus on the Damascus road. It changed his life for ever (Romans 6:6 and Isaiah 43:18 tells us not to look on the things of the past, but to leave it behind. Paul could have stayed in his shame, and never walked forward into his future with God.

1 John 1:9 is a promise from God that says if we are sorry for our own sins, then we are forgiven and cleansed from all unrighteousness. So we should let them go, forget them, because our record is clear. Justified – just as if I'd never sinned!

God's grace covers it all. All our sin and shame. Jesus died on the cross and took all our sin on Himself. He did it for you and for me – for every sin we would ever commit in our lifetime. He carried it all for us.

As we say sorry for our sin, and ask Jesus into our lives, He makes us a brand-new person in Christ with a new heart and new desires.

We are now on the journey with God, and our perspective in life has changed. Our perspective in ourselves has also changed. We have a desire to please God and do His will. We have become Born Again, and we *know* we are going to heaven when we leave this earth. God has forgotten our sins (Hebrews 8:12)! We are learning to trust Him to lead us and guide us through life (Hebrews 7:25).

God now sees us "in Jesus," washed in His blood and clothed in His righteousness. Jesus represents us before the throne of God, and lives to intercede for us before the Father.

2. Our minds must be renewed

Romans 12:2: *And do not be conformed to this world, but be transformed by the renewing of your mind, so that you may prove what the will of God is, that which is good and acceptable and perfect.*

If we want to grow spiritually, then we need to meditate on the Word of God as often as we can. Meditation is like thinking about something and dwelling on it. We fill our minds with it. We turn it over in our minds. The Word of God is active, and it will help us in our thinking, and in our mindsets that need changing.

2 Timothy 3:16-17: *All Scripture is inspired by God and profitable for teaching, for reproof, for correction, for training in righteousness; so that the man of God may be adequate, equipped for every good work.*

We are all at different stages of growth, so we need to go at our own pace, and do what we can do now. Perhaps start with reading one verse, and remember it throughout the day. This will strengthen us. Then we can build from that gradually. The Holy Spirit will help us as we turn the Word of God over in our minds. He will help us to understand it, and put our faith in its truth. We need to be consistent as much as we can, but not feel guilty if we miss sometimes. It's not legalism – it's relationship with Jesus (1 Timothy 4:15)!

Our thought-life is very important. We should have some Scripture in our minds as we go into our day. Then we can reflect on it at any time, and gain strength from it. This is how our minds get renewed and we grow spiritually (Proverbs 23:7).

What we think, we are! If we want to see things from a different perspective we need to get more of God's Word into us. Some of the greatest growth and changes will come through God's Word at work in us (Psalm 19:9-14).

3. Heartfelt prayer

Matthew 6:6-8: Jesus said, *"But you, when you pray, go into your inner room, close your door and pray to your Father who is in secret, and your Father who sees what is done in secret will reward you. And when you are praying, do not use meaningless repetition as the Gentiles do, for they suppose that they will be heard for their many words. So do not be like them; for your Father knows what you need before you ask Him."*

When we are praying from our hearts, we are connecting deeply with God. The Holy Spirit brings things to our minds that may be hidden from others, and sometimes we have not been aware of this. He shows us the truth about ourselves, and things we need to confess and change (2 Corinthians 4:2).

The Holy Spirit convicts us where it's needed, so that we can be cleansed and corrected. We realise that without Him we cannot do anything, and realise how dependent we are on Him and His presence in our lives. God hears our cries and answers us.

In the place of prayer we become aware of God's purposes for our lives, and we can see our vision and our dream being born. We are being transformed by His Holy Spirit. As we focus on Jesus we are being changed from one degree of glory to another (2 Corinthians 3:18).

Prayer calls on God to do what is impossible for man. Paul wrote *"Pray without ceasing"* (1 Thessalonians 5:17).

Jesus' whole life and ministry began and ended with prayer. Even when the crowds were pressing on Him, He withdrew to pray to His Father. Why? Because He knew His source of power. If He needed prayer, how much more do we! In Luke 6:12 we read that Jesus spent all night praying. Prayer changes our focus and our perspective.

4. Knowing who we are in Christ

Ephesians 2:4-6: *But God, being rich in mercy, because of His great love with which He loved us, even when we were dead in our transgressions, made us alive together with Christ (by grace you have been saved), and raised us up with Him, and seated us with Him in the heavenly places in Christ Jesus.*

We have been raised up! And we sit with Him in the Heavenly Places. Everything that Jesus has, we also have. Our inheritance is in Christ (Ephesians 1:13-23).

We rule and reign with Him (Philippians 4:13 and Romans 8:37). The enemy is under our feet (James 4:7). When we submit to God and resist the devil, he has to go! God has given us Authority and Power in the Name of Jesus (Luke 9:1-2). He has given us the keys of the Kingdom (Matthew 16:19).

We have Power and Authority and Dominion in our sphere of influence. Satan always tells us lies. He tells us we have no power. He tries to convince us that he has all the power. It is God who is the All Powerful One, and we are called to reign in life by Christ Jesus (Romans 5:17).

We are kings and priests unto our God (Revelation 1:4-6 and 5:9-10). We have the Kingdom of God living in us. We are the expression of the Kingdom on earth – an expression of His love, His power, His authority, His peace and His joy, His abundant life and His presence.

When we recognise who we are in Jesus, then our perspective will change in the way we see circumstances, in the way we see others, and in the way we see ourselves. We need to feel good about ourselves, about what God has placed within us (2 Corinthians 4:7).

If we don't love ourselves, then we can feel insecure and dependent on others for approval. It then becomes hard to reach our full potential or to love others. God loves us and accepts us as we are. If we don't believe and receive that fact, then we live feeling insecure, disagreeing with God.

Maybe we need to ask for fresh a revelation of God's love for us. What we feel about ourselves, other people will sense when they are around us.

Our opinion of *ourselves* needs to be based on *God's* opinion of us. This means not thinking too highly of ourselves, but recognising that we are totally loved and accepted by God, and our security is in Him alone. So instead of putting ourselves down, we need to recognise the treasure within us that God has put there.

5. Say what God says

Proverbs 18:21: *Death and life are in the power of the tongue, And those who love it will eat its fruit.*

We must be careful not to say things that go against God's Word, but to come in agreement with it. As we speak the truth of God Word, we are speaking life and power over situations and over ourselves and others. It is good to think about what we say before we say it!

We need to speak blessings over ourselves and others (Isaiah 65:16). What we say, influences us and others, and also influences our moods and our day. Our whole lives are influenced by what we say. Our words are powerful – they have the power of life and death.

Our direction and our perspective in life and situations are affected by what we say, by what we think, and by what we do. Jabez spoke blessing over himself (1 Chronicles 4:10).

Jabez asked God for blessing, enlargement and protection, and for God's hand to be with him. And God gave him his request.

We need to be careful not to speak negatives over ourselves, such as, "I'm a failure. I will never amount to anything etc.)

Coming into agreement with God's Word, we can repeat Paul's words in Philippians 4:13, "I can do all things through Him who strengthens me!"

Speak words of truth, life and wholeness (Proverbs 6:2).

6. Hunger for and pursue God's Presence more

Matthew 5:6: Jesus said, *"Blessed are those who hunger and thirst for righteousness, for they shall be satisfied."*

If we feel in a rut with our relationship with God, we need to work on the time we spend in His presence. Intimacy with God is all-important for our growth – and for our right perspective spiritually.

Time spent just being with Him in His presence, worshipping Him, telling Him we love Him, and drawing close to hear His voice through our thoughts, through His Word, and in our spirits. Again, it is not legalism, it is relationship with Jesus – and it grows and develops over time.

As we discipline ourselves to spend time with Him, the Holy Spirit will help us and we will want to be in His presence more, and our hunger and desire for God will grow.

We must come into alignment with Him everyday with His will for us, following the leading of the Holy Spirit. We must get rid of hindrances that stop us getting that quality time with God. Maybe we need to say No to some things. Or maybe finish with something that we have been doing for a long time, if God shows us to.

Our perspective and our focus can so easily get off centre. *Jesus* always needs to be the centre. The more time we spend with Him, the closer we will be to Him, and the more we will hear His voice. Every day is the day the Lord has made. We need to rejoice and be glad in it, or we will miss the beauty of the moments with God, no matter whatever or wherever that is (John 17:13).

Jesus wants us to have joy! He prayed for it, and God rejoices over us with singing (Zephaniah 3:17). He wants us to enjoy His company. Jesus is the Vine, and He wants us to abide – to stay and dwell with Him – to bring forth much fruit (John 15:1-5).

7. God is everything we need

Romans 8:32: *He who did not spare His own Son, but delivered Him over for us all, how will He not also with Him freely give us all things?*

There is no lack in God! He is more than enough. He is our provider, He will give us all that we need. Then *"Goodness and loving kindness will follow me all the days of my life"* (Psalm 23:6).

We need to stir up our faith and see that the impossible *is* possible. We need to raise the level of our expectation, to think, to speak, and act in faith. The more we feed our faith, the stronger it will be. Faith comes by hearing, and hearing by the Word of Christ (Romans 10:17).

We cannot please God without faith (Hebrews 11:6). We need to be willing for change in our lives if we want to grow. If we want our faith to increase, we need to have a goal that's beyond our comfort zone, and stretches our faith.

We all have a measure of faith. Jude 20 tells us to build ourselves up in our most holy faith. 2 Thessalonians 1:3-4 tells us how the church in Thessalonica was in the midst of persecution, and yet their faith was being greatly enlarged, and their love was growing. How wonderful! There perspective seemed to be right, and in the middle of their affliction they were enduring. Their focus was in the right place.

1 Corinthians 3:21-23: *So then let no one boast in men. For all things belong to you, whether Paul or Apollos or Cephas or the world or life or death or things present or things to come; all things belong to you, and you belong to Christ; and Christ belongs to God.*

A prayer to ask Jesus into your life – if you would like to

Dear Lord Jesus, I thank You for dying on the cross for me. I'm sorry for all the wrong things I've done in my life. Please forgive me. Come into my life. Fill me with Your Holy Spirit, and make me a brand-new person in You.

Thank You, Jesus. Amen.

A general prayer

Dear Lord Jesus, help me to have the right perspective in my life. Help me to renew my mind with Your Word, and to know heartfelt prayer and intimacy with You.

Help me to know who I am in You and all that I have in You. Help me to think, speak and act in agreement with You and Your Word. Increase my hunger for You, and increase my faith to believe the impossible!

Fill me afresh with Your Holy Spirit, and help me to see myself as You see me, and to know that my security is in You alone.

In Jesus' Name. Amen.

18. Seven Truths about Brokenness

From this Chapter

We all need to be broken to become more like Jesus. If we partake in His glory, we must be willing to partake in His sufferings. This is how God prepares us and equips us for greater fruitfulness in His Kingdom. Without brokenness in our lives, we cannot share the fragrance of Jesus in the most effective way – because we get in the way! We need to decrease, and He needs to increase, then something will emerge in our lives that is beautiful for God.

1. The trial of our faith

1 Peter 1:6-7: *In this you greatly rejoice, even though now for a little while, if necessary, you have been distressed by various*

trials, so that the proof of your faith, being more precious than gold which is perishable, even though tested by fire, may be found to result in praise and glory and honor at the revelation of Jesus Christ.

God forms the character of Jesus Christ in us through difficult times. When things become hard, don't believe the lie that God is distracted. At these times, and all the time, God is very much at work in us – refining us and breaking us, so we depend on Him even more!

We all need to be broken to become more like Jesus. If we partake in His glory, we must be willing to partake in His sufferings. This is how God prepares us and equips us for greater fruitfulness in His Kingdom.

Without brokenness in our lives, we cannot share the fragrance of Jesus in the most effective way – because we get in the way! We need to decrease, and He needs to increase.

We need to be purified to grow spiritually. There is always blessing on the other side of the trial. God uses these things for our good, to mature and develop us. And while we are in the trial, Jesus is right there with us. We are promised that the "rivers" will not overflow us (Isaiah 43:2).

We learn our greatest lessons in the valley. When things look really bad, God is still a good God. We choose our attitudes in every situation. Our response in the hard places of life can determine if we gain from the experience – or lose from it. God always wants us to gain from it.

2. We need to die to self

Galatians 2:20: *I have been crucified with Christ; and it is no longer I who live, but Christ lives in me; and the life which I now live in the flesh I live by faith in the Son of God, who loved me and gave Himself up for me.*

Paul said, "*May it never be that I would boast, except in the cross of our Lord Jesus Christ* (Galatians 6:14). The only way to heaven is through the cross. There are no shortcuts or alternatives.

Hebrews 9:22: *And according to the Law, one may almost*

say, all things are cleansed with blood, and without shedding of blood there is no forgiveness.

It is only when we humble ourselves at the foot of the cross that we can be transformed from death to newness of life. When Jesus died on the cross, He dealt with the devil, sin, and self. The cross of Jesus changes our perspective on life. When Jesus died for us, we died with Him. Romans 6:11: *Even so consider yourselves to be dead to sin, but alive to God in Christ Jesus.*

Now we live in Him and in newness of life, power, and strength by His Holy Spirit (Philippians 4:13). We cannot do anything in our own strength. It just becomes self-effort, because it is rooted in self. We need to get out of the way so the Holy Spirit can fully have *His* way.

It is death before life, death before power, and death before fruit. In the impossibilities of life, and in the trials of life, we can trust God's promises. They never fail. We can lean and depend on Him, and He will come through for us.

We need to be willing to be made conformable to His death – daily (Philippians 3:10). In this way, rivers of Living Water will flow from us to the needy world (John 7:38).

3. Commitment that is radical

Luke 9:23: *He was saying to them all, "If anyone wishes to come after Me, he must deny himself, and take up his cross daily and follow Me."*

We have to turn from our self-life and our selfish desires. Jesus has not called us to be lukewarm (Revelation 3:16). We are called to put "self" on the altar daily, to take up our cross and follow Him – to fully enter in to what already has been done on the cross! We don't then follow our own wishes and desires, but we follow *Him*, and go where *He* leads – and do as *He* says.

We need to allow Him to break us, melt us, mould us, and fill us with His Holy Spirit afresh daily, renewing our minds with the Word of God (Romans 12:2).

The more we let go of what we want, the more we will desire and hunger after God – the more we will grow spiritually. What kind of fruit is growing in our lives? Are we becoming more fixed to the things of earth, or becoming more like Jesus? It's good to reflect and examine what fruit is in our lives.

If it's good fruit, that is something to thank God for. But we are not to become complacent. But if we are not bearing good fruit, then we need to put it right with God straight away, and focus on the right things. We are chosen to bring forth *good fruit* for the Kingdom.

John 15:5: *"I am the vine, you are the branches; he who abides in Me and I in him, he bears much fruit, for apart from Me you can do nothing."*

Jesus is the Master Gardener. He prunes us for greater fruitfulness. He cuts off things that stop us growing and bearing more fruit. He will cut back certain things in our lives, so that we will bring forth much fruit. We just need to be willing, so we will be the best we can be for His glory.

4. Keep a clear conscience before God

Acts 24:16: In court for his faith, Paul told the governor, *I also do my best to maintain always a blameless conscience both before God and before men.*

We must always listen and obey the clear promptings of the Holy Spirit in our lives. It may be a warning, or some choice we have made that is wrong and we need to put it right. We need to be teachable and stay humble. We need to watch our motives. Ask ourselves why do we do certain things. If we feel we may have hurt someone, we need to ask their forgiveness.

Ask the Holy Spirit to reveal any changes we need to make in our lives. We need to love and honour others, and put them before ourselves. We must put right any wrong thoughts, to confess them, and take them captive under the blood of Jesus in obedience to Him (2 Corinthians 10:5).

We must always keep short accounts with God, and keep our hearts and lives right before Him and others, always looking for the good in others, and encouraging them in their calling and vision. We need to believe in them and in what God has placed within them. We mustn't think of ourselves more highly then we ought to, but know who we are and what we have in Jesus.

It is important to be thankful for all that God has done for us, and is still doing as He works within us by His Holy Spirit to make us more and more like Jesus.

5. We share in His glory and His sufferings

1 Peter 2:21: *For you have been called for this purpose, since Christ also suffered for you, leaving you an example for you to follow in His steps.*

We need to make Jesus Lord of our lives. Many have quoted this phrase, "If Jesus is not Lord of all, He is not Lord at all!"

As Jesus is Lord in our lives, then we must allow Him to rule and reign in every area. There is only room for one on the throne of our hearts. The Lordship of Jesus has to touch every detail of our lives. He is our Potter, and we are the clay. We have to let Him shape us according to His will, and His plan and purpose for us.

Jesus makes us into something beautiful for His glory! He makes us vessels fit for His use, to be a blessing to others. During the process we will experience things we don't understand – we all do at times. But God is working for our good, always for our good to make us the best that we can be for His glory.

We are called to be His servants, and to serve others in love. We are made to be conformed to His image (Romans 8:29). Jesus gave everything, so we would be with Him for ever, and no longer live for ourselves.

2 Corinthians 5:13-15: *For if we are beside ourselves, it is for God; if we are of sound mind, it is for you. For the love of Christ controls us, having concluded this, that one died for all, therefore all died; and He died for all, so that they who live might no longer live for themselves, but for Him who died and rose again on their behalf.*

Jesus is our example. Hebrews 5:8 tells us that although He was God's only Son, He learned obedience by the things He suffered.

Romans 8:16-18: *The Spirit Himself testifies with our spirit that we are children of God, and if children, heirs also, heirs of God and fellow heirs with Christ, if indeed we suffer with Him so that we may also be glorified with Him. For I consider that the sufferings of this present time are not worthy to be compared with the glory that is to be revealed to us.*

6. The fragrance of the alabaster box

Mark 14:3-6: *While He was in Bethany at the home of Simon the leper, and reclining at the table, there came a woman with an alabaster vial of very costly perfume of pure nard; and she broke the vial and poured it over His head. But some were indignantly remarking to one another, "Why has this perfume been wasted? For this perfume might have been sold for over three hundred denarii, and the money given to the poor." And they were scolding her. But Jesus said, "Let her alone; why do you bother her? She has done a good deed to Me."*

Some of them called it "a waste!" But Jesus told them to leave the woman alone, and He highly commended her for what she had done. The woman came to display her love for Jesus, and anointed Him for His burial. She didn't care who was watching her. She worshipped Him and anointed Him with the most expensive perfume she could find. She was busy making much of Jesus. As she broke the box, the fragrance must have filled the house. It was an act of worship.

The more we are broken, the more the fragrance of Jesus is released wherever we go. We carry the fragrance of the Holy Spirit. Jesus took bread and broke it, and blessed it (Luke 24:30). That is what God does in our lives. Sometimes God takes us through situations to increase our dependence on Him, and to keep us humble, blessed and broken for His service.

Our flesh must be crucified daily. Are we ready to be that living sacrifice on the altar of His service? (Matthew 16:24-25).

Philippians 2:17-18: *But even if I am being poured out as a drink offering upon the sacrifice and service of your faith, I rejoice and share my joy with you all. You too, I urge you, rejoice in the same way and share your joy with me..*

Paul says how glad he is to be offered up as a sacrifice and offering for the people. So he encourages them to be happy too. He was willing to give himself for them. He was rejoicing in their faith in the cross.

7. That I may know Him

Philippians 3:10-11: ... *that I may know Him and the power of His resurrection and the fellowship of His sufferings, being conformed to His death; in order that I may attain to the resurrection from the dead.*

In this verse Paul is talking about knowing the power of Jesus' resurrection, and the fellowship of His sufferings. If we really want to know Jesus, we need to be prepared to share in His sufferings – however that works out in our lives. It will mean something different for each one of us, but God always promises to be in it with us and give us that special grace in that time of need.

We must always let the hard times in our lives take us to the secret place. It is there in the place of intimacy that we prove God's power in our lives. Things happen in the place of intimacy that cannot happen anywhere else. That is why His Presence must have top priority in our lives (Isaiah 40:31). We must wait for His Presence, listen for His voice, and give Him quality time – time to receive from Him, to be refreshed, restored, built up and strengthened by the power of the Holy Spirit.

Time with God is never wasted – it is always productive in our lives. Romans 12:1 speaks of us as living sacrifices. The sacrifice is always found on the altar – nothing held back. In Romans 12:1 Paul calls it our "spiritual service of worship."

Philippians 1:21: *For to me, to live is Christ and to die is gain.*

A Prayer

Help me, Lord, to give Your Holy Spirit permission to "break me" and make me that "living sacrifice" on the altar for You. Help me to know that I am dead to sin and alive to You! (Romans 6:11)

Help me to walk in newness of life. May the fragrance of Jesus flow from me to affect other lives for good – and for God, my Heavenly Father.

Help me to renew my mind through Your Word daily, to

make me a blessing to others. Mature me, and develop me in You.

Draw me closer to You, so I will know what it means to be that "living sacrifice." I humble myself before You, in dependence on Your Holy Spirit to make me all You want me to be.

In Jesus' Name. Amen.

19. Seven Ways to be Resilient

Inside this Chapter

Resilient people see setbacks and giants in the land as something they can conquer! Something that can bring them into greatness, rather than taking away what they already have! In Numbers 13 the spies see the giants as something bigger than God – something they cannot overcome. Caleb and Joshua did not share their negativity. They knew they could conquer them. They knew that their God was bigger than the greatest thing they could ever come up against. They knew that they were well able to conquer these giants and take the land.

1. Setbacks can bring us into greatness
Proverbs 24:15-16: *Do not lie in wait, O wicked man, against the dwelling of the righteous; Do not destroy his resting place; For a righteous man falls seven times, and rises again, But the wicked stumble in time of calamity.*

Resilient people see setbacks and giants in the land as something they can conquer! Something that can bring them into greatness, rather than taking away what they already have! In Numbers 13 the spies see the giants as something bigger than God – something they cannot overcome.

Caleb and Joshua did not share their negativity. They knew they could conquer them. They knew that their God was bigger than the greatest thing they could ever come up against. They knew that they were well able to conquer these giants and take the land.

However many times we fall, however many obstacles we encounter, resilience will cause us to rise again and say, "Just one more time." And we need to say it every time we encounter obstacles (2 Corinthians 11:23-33.) We read in these verses from this letter to the Corinthian church about the endurance and resilience of Paul. In all the desperate times he went through, he never gave up!

2. Embrace trials

James 1:2-4: *Consider it all joy, my brethren, when you encounter various trials, knowing that the testing of your faith produces endurance. And let endurance have its perfect result, so that you may be perfect and complete, lacking in nothing.*

James tells us to welcome trials, and be happy! If we are resilient, we won't just face trials, but we will embrace them because we will understand that they produce fruit – good things – in us that we cannot achieve in any other way.

There are no shortcuts with God, but he always works things together for our good (1 Peter 4:12-13). We may go through many trials and difficulties in life, but God never lets us down, and never lets us go. He is always there with us, giving us all that we need. He walks with us through dark valleys and delivers us (Psalm 34:19).

In 2 Corinthians 12:7-10 Paul speaks about his "thorn" that God didn't take away. God tells him that His grace is sufficient for him. Paul proved that God's strength showed up greater through his weakness – showed him that he was glad to be a living demonstration of God's power living in him through his weakness.

Paul was happy about his hardships and difficulties, because he knew that when he was weak then the more he depended on God, then the stronger he was.

The more we depend on God, the more His power shows up, and the more He is glorified through us.

3. Be a God pleaser

Proverbs 29:25: *The fear of man brings a snare, but he who trusts in the Lord will be exalted.*

Trying to please people all the time brings us into all kinds of traps. Pleasing God should be our main aim in life. Living to please Him sets us free from bondage. Every day we need to be grateful to God in prayer for all that He is, and all that He has done – and all that He is going to do.

An attitude of gratitude creates an atmosphere of faith in our lives – and faith overcomes fear and unbelief. We need to be expectant for what God is going to do, to come into alignment with what God is doing in our lives every day; to be obedient to His instructions.

Our destiny is fulfilled just one day at a time. What we do daily is the sum total of our lifestyle and our destiny. We must make sure our focus is on Him and on pleasing Him. Our strength is there, our joy is there, our everything we need is there – in God Himself.

If we feel afraid, we need to speak out and declare the Word of God and His promises in the face of the enemy. Our words have power, so we need to be careful what we say (Proverbs 18:21).

We have the power in us to talk, act, and think – according to the Word of God.

4. Live in the present

2 Peter 3:11-13: *Since all these things are to be destroyed in this way, what sort of people ought you to be in holy conduct and godliness, looking for and hastening the coming of the day of*

God, because of which the heavens will be destroyed by burning, and the elements will melt with intense heat! But according to His promise we are looking for new heavens and a new earth, in which righteousness dwells.

God is the "Great I Am" not "I was" or "I will be." Our greatest influence is in the moment, today where we are. We will never come this way again, never have this particular day again or the same moment. So it's good for us to make the most of this day, this time that we have now.

We need to know the manna (God's provision) for this day, to know what God is giving us, what He is saying to us, and how He is leading us. We need to be leaving the past behind, not worrying about the future, living to the "full" in the "Now" with God, proving Him to be who He says He is, to be entering into all that God has today for us.

Are we praising Him, trusting Him, studying His Word? Praying, communicating with Him, listening to Him, waiting on Him? Are we making much of Him?

With God there is never an occasion for marking time. God is never doing *nothing*. He is always doing something. He never stops working on our behalf. So we must use today well in the purpose of God.

5. Know that all things are possible

John 10:29: *My Father, who has given them to Me, is greater than all; and no one is able to snatch them out of the Father's hand.*

When things look hopeless, there is always a way forward with God (Psalm 42:11). When dreams have not been fulfilled but seem to have been shattered, God's purpose for us stays intact. He turns our setbacks into His opportunities.

Jesus hears and understands our heartaches. He has been there before! We can be real with God. He knows us anyway. We can come in total safety and security, and He will help and heal us. Yes, God will come through in wonderful ways.

In painful times we can still have faith in God, and receive His guidance and instruction (Psalm 40:1-3). When we don't get the answer we want in the way we want it, it is harder to believe God's promises. But that is the time to press into God more than ever! To trust Him in what He gives us, and also in what He doesn't give us. Everything God does is for our own good.

6. Visualize victory

2 Chronicles 20:22-23: *When they began singing and praising, the Lord set ambushes against the sons of Ammon, Moab and Mount Seir, who had come against Judah; so they were routed. For the sons of Ammon and Moab rose up against the inhabitants of Mount Seir destroying them completely; and when they had finished with the inhabitants of Seir, they helped to destroy one another.*

The word came to Jehoshaphat not to be afraid. The battle is not His but God's – verse 15. Jehoshaphat told the people, "Believe in the Lord your God and you will have success. Believe His prophets, and everything will be all right" – verse 20.

Jehoshaphat saw the victory before it came! If we can see it by faith, we will have it. Abraham counted the stars, and believed God that His promise would come to pass. And it did (Hebrews 11:11-12)! See also Mark 11:24 and Hebrews 11:1.

Elijah saw the rain before one drop began to fall. So he prepared. He cut out all distractions so he could pray for rain. He saw it coming. He believed and prepared. Elijah was single-minded and expectant. He believed by faith and didn't give up. He sent his servant out seven times to look!

Noah believed God when he built the Ark on dry ground. He activated his faith. God increases our faith in times like these. God uses prepared people and expectant people.

7. Reflect regularly

2 Chronicles 29:5: Hezekiah said, *"Listen to me, O Levites. Consecrate yourselves now, and consecrate the house of the LORD, the God of your fathers, and carry the uncleanness out from the holy place.*

Spiritual growth is essential, and we need to reflect regularly regarding where we stand with God. What is the fruit of our lives? What are our attitudes, our motives, our character, our behaviour? We need to be displaying the Fruit of the Spirit (Galatians 5).

We need to know what God wants us to keep and what He wants us to let go. We need to keep our "temples" clean and clear of clutter. We are the temples of the Holy Spirit. In our natural houses things can creep in over time that need clearing out. In our temples things can get cluttered and get out of perspective and off centre.

We need to get back on track, to clear foggy vision, to let go of even good things in order to receive the best. We must use our gifts, but recognise that it is our fruit that we are known by. Our character is the total of our daily habits. We need integrity, and honour those who walk in truth. We need to keep our promises, and stay away from gossip. The person who does these things will never be shaken.

Psalm 15: *O Lord, who may abide in Your tent? Who may dwell on Your holy hill? He who walks with integrity, and works righteousness, And speaks truth in his heart. He does not slander with his tongue, Nor does evil to his neighbor, Nor takes up a reproach against his friend; In whose eyes a reprobate is despised, But who honors those who fear the Lord; He swears to his own hurt and does not change; He does not put out his money at interest, Nor does he take a bribe against the innocent. He who does these things will never be shaken.*

A Prayer

Dear Lord Jesus, will You help me to understand setbacks and trials in the way You want me to? Help me to embrace them and trust You in them. Make me resilient in You and Your purposes. Help me to prove Your strength in my weakness. Help me to please You and not be in fear of man.

Teach me to talk, think and act in a way that glorifies You. Help me to make the most of my time here. Let me find my total security and safety in You. Increase my faith and my trust in You. And help me to deal with any clutter in my life.

In Jesus' Name. Amen.

20. Seven Truths about Reflection

Inside this Chapter

Reflection is remembering, pondering, recalling the goodness of our God. As we remember and reflect on His goodness, His grace, and His mercy in our lives, we need to be thankful and grateful.

There is a big difference between reflecting on past things in a positive way and thanking God for them, and dwelling on the past in a negative way and being stuck there. So let it go! The Holy Spirit will help us if we are willing. He will support us, guide us, and supply us with all that we need.

1. Reflect on the good things

Deuteronomy 32:11: *Like an eagle that stirs up its nest, that hovers over its young, He spread His wings and caught them, He carried them on His pinions.*

Reflect on God – Father, Son and Holy Spirit. Reflect on the good things He has done in our lives, the ways in which He has spoken to us, and blessed and encouraged us.

Reflection is remembering, pondering, recalling the goodness of our God. As we remember and reflect on His goodness, His grace, and His mercy in our lives, we need to be thankful and grateful.

Some lines of the worship song by Bethel Music go, "All my life You have been faithful, all my life You have been so, so good; With every breath that I am able, I will sing of the goodness of God."

Reflect on how God has kept us by His power, how He has led us all the way. Reflect how He has used our gifts as we have given them to Him, and used them to bless others. Reflect how He has protected us when we haven't been aware of it, how He has picked us up when we have fallen.

Reflect how He has allowed us to be unashamed through His great love and mercy and kindness. Reflect how He knows the worst about us, and yet loves us the most – more than anyone else does!

We need to reflect how Jesus is before the Father night and day, standing up for us, interceding for us. Jesus is reminding the Father that we are covered by His blood. We need to reflect how He has sheltered us under His wings, and teaches us to fly and soar with Him. Jesus loves us too much to leave us where we are. He always wants to see us grow spiritually and move on with Him. He never gives up on us, is never disappointed in us, and He is never a disappointment to us.

We have so much to thank God for. David looked back and remembered and reflected on how God had helped him in the past as he faced Goliath, how God has saved him from the lion and the bear, and how He will save him now and give him the victory over this giant. And He did! (1 Samuel 17:37).

2. Reflect on the harder things

John 14:27: *Peace I leave with you; My peace I give to you; not as the world gives do I give to you. Do not let your heart be troubled, nor let it be fearful.*

As Jesus goes to be with the Father, so He gives us the Comforter, the Holy Spirit (John 14:16). The Holy Spirit lives in every believer, and is powerful and always with us to help us to handle hardships and difficulties. He keeps us by His power, and gives us peace in the storm. Reflect how faithful God is, when sometimes we are not; how He instructs us in the valley and restores our soul.

As we remember and reflect on the harder times in our lives, let us do this in a positive way so we can always move forward with God. If there are things that are not yet dealt with from the past, then it is good to put them right as far as we can, so they can be resolved with God and others if necessary. Repent if we have to, and forgive if we need to. Sometimes we have to go back in order to move on.

We can then look back and remember and reflect in a positive way, knowing that wrong things are dealt with, and understanding those things that we have learnt through these situations and circumstances in our lives. The memory of the past can trap us if we let it.

There is a big difference between reflecting on past things in a positive way and thanking God for them, and dwelling on the past in a negative way and being stuck there. So let it go! The Holy Spirit will help us if we are willing. He will support us, guide us, and supply us with all that we need.

Romans 8:14: *For all who are being led by the Spirit of God, these are sons of God.*

3. Reflect on our lifestyle

Psalm 71:15: *My mouth shall tell of Your righteousness and of Your salvation all day long; for I do not know the sum of them.*

It's good to reflect on our daily lifestyle. For example, why do we do what we do? What do we need to give up? What takes most of our time? Are we burnt out? Have we taken on too much? Do

breadth and length and height and depth, and to know the love of Christ which surpasses knowledge, that you may be filled up to all the fullness of God.

5. Reflect on His sacrifice

1 Corinthians 11:23-24: *For I received from the Lord that which I also delivered to you, that the Lord Jesus in the night in which He was betrayed took bread; and when He had given thanks, He broke it and said, "This is My body, which is for you; do this in remembrance of Me."*

Every time we come to take the bread and the wine, we are remembering and reflecting on Jesus' great sacrifice for us on the cross (Romans 5:8). As we reflect and remember, it's good to recall what we used to be like before Jesus changed our lives, before we were born again by His Spirit. This kind of reflecting will keep us humble and well-balanced, especially as we share our faith with others (1 Timothy 1:15-16).

Isaiah 51:1: *Listen to me, you who pursue righteousness, who seek the Lord: Look to the rock from which you were hewn and to the quarry from which you were dug.*

This once-and-for-all sacrifice paid the price for all our sins from the cradle to the grave. Jesus took our blame and our sin on Himself, so we can be freed from the power and tyranny of it. So we can have the choice how we live.

We are all sinners, and we all need a Saviour, but we all have freedom of choice. We choose life – or we choose death. What we need to do is choose Jesus, say sorry for our sin, and receive His free gift of salvation by faith. Then we can know we are going to heaven when we leave this earth.

We can't earn this. Salvation is a *free gift*, and we just need to accept it, to put our trust in Jesus and surrender our lives to Him, ask Him into our hearts and receive His gift of eternal life. Then we will know that all is right between us and Him!

Jesus forgives all our sin. He has cleared our record, paid in full! (Colossians 2:14). Our true identity lies in our relationship with Jesus, not on what *we* have done or what *we* are doing. It is in Him that we find our true selves. It is in Him that we find our true value and worth. If we look to others to determine our worth, we will be disappointed. Pleasing people is a trap that ensnares us (Proverbs 29:25 and Galatians 1:10). We are loved and approved of by God, and *that* is what really matters.

6. Reflect on what God has spoken to us

Acts 20:35: *In everything I showed you that by working hard in this manner you must help the weak and remember the words of the Lord Jesus, that He Himself said, 'It is more blessed to give than to receive.'*

Keep a journal of our journey with Him, to remind ourselves of things He has spoken into our lives at different times and seasons. Where we need to, we must be obedient to what God is saying to us, to encourage ourselves with those prophetic words He has given us. But we must always remember to weigh them in the light of God's Word which is infallible. We need to remember and reflect on a portion of the Word of God through which God has spoken to us very powerfully.

We need to remind ourselves of confirmations He has given us on certain issues, and things that we are still waiting on Him for. This reminds us and teaches us to wait patiently and well, to be constant in prayer, and believing in faith and expectancy for God's clarity to come in His timing.

If we have a vision from God, we must remind ourselves to keep it alive and speak life into it, that the vision will live. We need to run with it, write it down, and by faith see it come to pass even before it does. We need to act on it, and be intentional in focus and goal – to remove any distractions.

Men and women of vision come into alignment with what God is doing. If we don't have a vision, we need to ask God for one! Where the fire has become dying embers, we need to fan the flame again! We need to use any dormant gift again, and as we do, it will blossom and ignite again and bless others.

Life is full of challenges and changes. God is stirring us up, disturbing the nest, teaching us to fly with Him. He is taking away our comfort zone, and like boats in the harbour, pushing us out to sea. So remember and reflect!

7. Reflect on a regular basis

Revelation 2:2-4: *"I know your deeds and your toil and perseverance, and that you cannot tolerate evil men, and you put to the test those who call themselves apostles, and they are not, and you found them to be false; and you have perseverance and have endured for My name's sake, and have not grown weary. But I have this against you, that you have left your first love."*

These verses remind us to keep sharp, on our toes, tuned into God. To remind us to return to our first love if we need to, and keep our cutting edge sharp. We are not to allow other things to take the place of our first love.

We have to prioritise and keep first things first. Our relationship with Jesus should be our *top priority*! That is why we need to remember and reflect as often as we can, to keep priorities in the right order.

We need to deal with past mistakes, regrets, grudges, hurt, anger, fear, isolation, resentment etc. This stuff will keep us stuck in the past. If we don't deal with it, we cannot move forward. We need to remember that we have an enemy, and he loves to see God's people trapped and stunted. But let us remember to and reflect on the fact that Jesus has won the victory over the enemy! He is a defeated foe!

We are not victims but victorious in Him. He has done it all, and for all time and eternity. The veil has been torn from top to bottom, and the way has been made for us to enter the Holy of Holies through His precious blood. We are *more* than conquerors! (Romans 8:37).

A Prayer

Before you pray, reflect on these words by the poet John Greenleaf Whittier (1807-1892): *For all sad words of tongue and pen, the saddest are these, "It might have been."*

In your later years will you look back with regret at unfulfilled God-given dreams? Or will you know that you have lived to fulfil your destiny? It's never too late with God to put things right and change direction!

Help me, Lord Jesus, to remember and reflect on a regular basis. Help me to deal with those things that need dealing with, to live my life in the right way with You. Teach me to reflect on my lifestyle and my growth, and to be sold out to You.

Set me free from people-pleasing, and let me live by my identity and worth in You alone. Set me on fire for You, that my relationship with You, Jesus, will have top priority in my life.

In Your name I pray, Amen.

A prayer if you would like to ask Jesus into your life

Lord Jesus, I thank You for dying on the cross for me, to take my sins away and give me a home in heaven.

I'm sorry for my sin, and I want to ask You, Jesus, to come into my life and make me a brand-new person in You.

I thank You for Your forgiveness.

In Jesus' Name. Amen.

21. Seven Ways to Grow

From this Chapter

Our decisions shape our lives. We make right choices and we make wrong choices. The choice we make is the difference between gaining and losing. We need to have right priorities in our lives. These will give us an idea where we will be with God in our future. They will point us in the right direction. Likewise, the wrong priorities will lead us in the wrong direction.

As we grow, God prunes us for our good and greater fruitfulness. He's not doing this for punishment. It's for greater effectiveness in the Kingdom. It is positive. We need to work with Him, so we gain and grow.

1. Put God First

Philippians 3:10-11: *...that I may know Him and the power of His resurrection and the fellowship of His sufferings, being conformed to His death; in order that I may attain to the resurrection from the dead.*

Paul made the decision to "live and walk in newness of life," whatever that meant for him. Growth is a decision we make. We must never doubt our ability to grow.

Our decisions shape our lives. We make right choices and we make wrong choices. The choice we make is the difference between gaining and losing.

We need to have right priorities in our lives. These will give us an idea where we will be with God in our future. They will point us in the right direction. Likewise, the wrong priorities will lead us in the wrong direction.

As we grow, God prunes us for our good and greater fruitfulness. He's not doing this for punishment. It's for greater effectiveness in the Kingdom. It is positive. We need to work with Him, so we gain and grow.

Watchman Nee wrote, "I have never met a soul who has set out to satisfy the Lord, and has not been satisfied himself!" Only God satisfies us. We will never find complete satisfaction in anything else. If we are looking for satisfaction in other things, we will be disappointed. Nothing satisfies us like God does. We were made by God for God, to worship Him and be in His presence for ever

2. Help and Support Others

Philippians 2:4: *Do not merely look out for your own personal interests, but also for the interests of others.*

We must not just be interested in ourselves, we *must* be interested in others. We need to believe in them, encourage them in their ministry and calling, and support them. As we do this, their confidence is built up in what God has given them. Knowing that someone believes in us, in what God has uniquely placed within us, causes us to fly!

If we are ignited, we will see others ignited in the Presence and Power of God. There will be increase in hunger for God, passion, a fresh touch of the Holy Spirit – desperation for more of God, pursuing Him. As we are stretched, others are stretched. As we grow, others grow. So our blessing is their blessing. As we refresh others, we also are refreshed

Proverbs 11:25: *The generous man will be prosperous, And he who waters will himself be watered.*

Giving is growing. The more we give to others, the more we grow. We need to build each other up. Proverbs 15:4: *A soothing tongue is a tree of life, But perversion in it crushes the spirit.*

We must speak helpful words. Proverbs 10:32: *The lips of the righteous bring forth what is acceptable, But the mouth of the wicked what is perverted.*

Words that we say can wound and crush someone's spirit. So let us encourage each other.

Joseph's brothers betrayed him. Joseph forgave them. He showed them grace and love and care. This is something we all need to receive, and we all need to give it to each other.

We need to show kindness, and acts of kindness to our enemies as well as to our friends and neighbours

3. We are Atmosphere Changers!

2 Corinthians 2:14-15: *But thanks be to God, who always leads us in triumph in Christ, and manifests through us the sweet aroma of the knowledge of Him in every place. For we are a fragrance of Christ to God among those who are being saved and among those who are perishing.*

As long as we speak negative words, we will reap negative lives. We won't experience victory. We need to remind ourselves that God is our source. Through Him we are victorious! We need to speak life and truth (2 Corinthians 3:18).

We reflect the glory of the Lord – like mirrors! The more we are in God's Presence, the more we reflect His Glory. We carry God's Presence with us (Matthew 5:16). We need to let our light shine.

God's Glory in us changes the atmosphere around us. We are the Light in the darkness. The light is meant to shine out and around, not to be hidden away. We need to walk in the Light as He is in the Light. No skeletons in the cupboard. No dark corners. Nothing left undone or un-dealt with.

Keep short accounts with God. No unconfessed sin (Psalm 32). There must be no doors of access for the enemy to take advantage of. No inroads for enemy activity in our lives.

If something is not in line with the Word of God, then leave it alone. We are living letters, seen and read by all people. Let our lives show His Glory, and display His Power, righteousness and truth.

Romans 14:17: *for the kingdom of God is not eating and drinking, but righteousness and peace and joy in the Holy Spirit.*

4. Keep Learning

Proverbs 1:5: *A wise man will hear and increase in learning, And a man of understanding will acquire wise counsel.*

If we read, we will learn and grow. None of us is past been taught! Growth and development come from being teachable.

As we read the Word of God prayerfully, the Holy Spirit teaches us and opens God's Word to us. God's Word should be the main book that we read. Why? Because it's like no other book. It is Living and sharp. It is Truth, and when mixed with our faith it activates within us to do us good. It is our daily spiritual food. As we feed on it, we will grow and be refreshed – convicted if necessary, blessed and built up.

The Word of God is a mirror that shows us who we really are. 2 Timothy 3:16-17: *All Scripture is inspired by God and profitable for teaching, for reproof, for correction, for training in righteousness; so that the man of God may be adequate, equipped for every good work.*

It is also good to read good Christian books to help us learn and grow spiritually. We can also learn from others who have moved on with God further than we have. It's good to be accountable to someone who is mature in God, and whom we can trust. It is good to learn from them in areas where we desire to move on, and become more effective and fruitful.

That is why it is important to listen and learn from others, and never become self-sufficient or proud. We need each other in the Body of Christ. We all have a special part that is vital in making up the whole body. Every part is essential for the functioning of the Body of Christ as one.

5. See Yourself Fulfilling Your Calling

Hebrews 11:8: *By faith Abraham, when he was called, obeyed by going out to a place which he was to receive for an inheritance; and he went out, not knowing where he was going.*

Think, talk, and see in faith. Moses kept his focus. His eye was on God – and he kept going. He kept going by faith, not by sight. If you can see yourself, by faith fulfilling your calling – you will!

In Hebrews 11 it was by faith that so many things were accomplished. Faith is the assurance of things hoped for, the conviction of things not seen (Hebrews 11:1).

Abraham's faith was counted as righteousness (Genesis 15:6). Without faith, it's impossible to please God (Hebrews 11:6).

Abraham believed against all the odds that God's promise would come to pass. He could see by faith as he counted the stars. Genesis 15:5: *And so shall your descendants be.*

Our vision and our calling should be greater than we are – far greater and unattainable without God. Way past our comfort zone. That which we can see "by faith" will come to pass. It is the assurance and conviction of things not yet seen with our natural eyes.

6. Have a Goal and Write it Down

Ephesians 5:16-17: *...making the most of your time, because the days are evil. So then do not be foolish, but understand what the will of the Lord is.*

We need to guard our minds and prioritise our time, to be single-minded, making the most of any chance we get to work towards seeing our vision come to pass. We must keep focused.

Broken focus is one of our greatest enemies, because it can catch us off guard. We need to keep clear of distractions. James

1:6-8: *But he must ask in faith without any doubting, for the one who doubts is like the surf of the sea, driven and tossed by the wind. For that man ought not to expect that he will receive anything from the Lord, being a double-minded man, unstable in all his ways.*

We must be determined to stay on track to see our vision and calling fulfilled. We must refuse negative thoughts and any influence which is not of God (Proverbs 4:23). We need to desire a deeper level of faith (Romans 1:17).

We need to seek God in everything, and get His guidance (Psalm 32:8), and align ourselves with God's will, and with the right people. We need to know God's will for our lives. As we seek Him, He will show us clearly (Psalm 143:10).

God's Word is a weapon – so use it against the enemy. Matthew 4:1-4: *Then Jesus was led up by the Spirit into the wilderness to be tempted by the devil. And after He had fasted forty days and forty nights, He then became hungry. And the tempter came and said to Him, "If You are the Son of God, command that these stones become bread." But He answered and said, "It is written, 'Man shall not live on bread alone, but on every word that proceeds out of the mouth of God.'"*

We must not be sidetracked. Sometimes we can be taken off track, even by good things. But if they are not what God is leading us into, the enemy will try to derail us into things that can take up a lot of time, where there is very little or no fruit.

These things can burn us out, which is why we need to stay in alignment with God's will and purpose for us.

7. Get Out of Your Comfort Zone

Deuteronomy 32:11: *Like an eagle that stirs up its nest, That hovers over its young, He spread His wings and caught them, He carried them on His pinions.*

Be ready and prepared for the unpredictable. We cannot put God in a box. We cannot expect Him to work in the same way every time. We need to be willing for God to take us to new levels with Him. This often means new ways of doing things – moving away from the old ways that did work, but don't work now. If we want to see change, we must be willing to let God change us and walk new ground with Him spiritually. We *can* take the Promised Land. We *can* reach our full potential and push away from the shore, from the safety of the harbour into the open sea.

We need to dream and stretch, reaching to go forward into the future and the calling that God has got for us. We need to listen to His voice, drink deeply at the well, and cry out to God for more. We must not settle for less than God's best. Don't restrict what God can do through us.

If we don't grow, we end up stuck in the same place with no change. We were *made* to grow! God is a God of increase. There is so much more with Him. We were made for enlargement, for new horizons. Whenever we try to move forward with God, we come up against obstacles and setbacks. We are in a battle – but the victory has been won! So we can overcome the obstacles in God's strength and power.

God told Joshua to be strong and of good courage (Joshua 1:9). That means "Don't give up!" God-given faith and courage will overcome every time. God wants to bring us into larger territory, and expand our vision.

How do we feel about where we are with God right now? To improve and grow means change. Isaiah 54:2: *"Enlarge the place of your tent; Stretch out the curtains of your dwellings, spare not; Lengthen your cords And strengthen your pegs."*

We need to take off the limits that we have put on ourselves, and be willing to go with God where we haven't been before. Our blessing and growth is someone else's blessing and growth! Maybe we need to fall in love with Jesus all over again?

Let's raise the level of our expectancy, to see beyond where we are right now. We must not settle for *less*, when there is so much *more*. We need to be willing to be stretched, in whatever way God wants to stretch us; to leave behind any hindrance, and not hold back. We need to take possession of the land God is giving us (Joshua 1:9).

A prayer, if you would like to use it:

Dear Lord, I give the Holy Spirit permission to stretch me and enlarge me. Take me to new levels with You, to raise the level of my expectancy and faith. Take me where I haven't been before, out of my comfort zone.

I want to allow You to make the changes in me that will make me fully on fire for You.

In Jesus' Name. Amen.

Something to reflect on:

* Don't settle for less than God's best.
* To give is to grow.
* Lift the limitations that we put on ourselves.
* Be willing to go beyond our comfort zone.
* We cannot improve *and* stay the same.
* What has to change in me to make me fully on fire for God?

22. Seven Truths about Angels

From this Chapter

Angels are messengers sent from God – to encourage, to warn, to prepare and show us the way. They turn up unexpectedly. Angels are looking out for us all the time (Matthew 18:10). Angels are ministering spirits (Hebrews 1:14). God sent an angel to deliver Peter from prison.

But we are not to worship angels. There is only One who is worthy of our worship. Only One True God. Only One on the Throne and in control. He is the One who has the last word, who knows the end from the beginning. God is the All Powerful One. There is no greater love than His love. No greater power than His power.

1. Angels are messengers and ministers

Acts 27:22-25: *Yet now I urge you to keep up your courage, for there will be no loss of life among you, but only of the ship. For this very night an angel of the God to whom I belong and whom I serve stood before me, saying, 'Do not be afraid, Paul; you must stand before Caesar; and behold, God has granted you all those who are sailing with you.' Therefore, keep up your courage, men, for I believe God that it will turn out exactly as I have been told.*

When Paul is on board the ship in a really bad storm, all hope is gone. A message comes from the angel to Paul, telling him not to fear. All the men with him will be saved, but they will lose the ship. So Paul encourages the crew that their lives will be saved. Angels are messengers sent from God – to encourage, to warn, to prepare and show us the way. They turn up unexpectedly. Angels are looking out for us all the time (Matthew 18:10). Angels are ministering spirits (Hebrews 1:14). God sent an angel to deliver Peter from prison.

Acts 12:7-10: *And behold, an angel of the Lord suddenly appeared and a light shone in the cell; and he struck Peter's side and woke him up, saying, "Get up quickly." And his chains fell off his hands. And the angel said to him, "Gird yourself and put on your sandals." And he did so. And he said to him, "Wrap your cloak around you and follow me."*

And he went out and continued to follow, and he did not know that what was being done by the angel was real, but thought he was seeing a vision. When they had passed the first and second guard, they came to the iron gate that leads into the city, which opened for them by itself; and they went out and went along one street, and immediately the angel departed from him.

The angel rescued Peter and set him free, but we must never forget that Jesus is far greater than the angels (Hebrews 1:3-6).

God sends His angels. The angels ministered to Jesus in Matthew 4:11. The Word of God tells us to be hospitable to strangers. They could be angels without us knowing it (Hebrews 13:2).

2. Angels protect us and provide for us

Psalm 91:11-12: *For He will give His angels charge concerning you, To guard you in all your ways. They will bear you up in their hands, That you do not strike your foot against a stone.*

When does God send His angels to help us? We can see examples of this in the Word of God. It may be when we feel let down by those who are close to us. In Genesis 21 we read about Hagar. Hagar felt let down by Abraham and Sarah when she was sent away with baby Ishmael with very little provision.

As she was crying, an angel called her and told her not to fear, because God had chosen him. Then she saw a well of water – an example of God's provision and protection in dry, hard places (Genesis 21:14-19).

Another example of angels helping is in giving God's protection in delivering us from our enemies. In Daniel 3:23-30 we read of three Hebrew young men who were thrown into the flaming furnace still tied up, because they wouldn't bow down to the King's statue.

As they looked, the people saw that the fire had no effect on them. They didn't even smell of smoke! The king and his officials saw that there was a fourth man in the fire with them. Then the King himself acknowledged the power of their God, and made a decree that no one shall speak evil of their God.

In verse 28 we see that the king blesses their God who has sent His angel and delivered the young men.

3. Angels bring help and show us the way

Psalm 34:7: *The angel of the Lord encamps around those who fear Him, And rescues them.*

God sends His angels to help us in troubled times. He rescues us. God sent angels to rescue Lot and his family. Lot obeyed God and lived, but his wife didn't obey so she perished (Genesis 19).

When there are great challenges in our lives, God sends His angels to help us. He sent a plan with His angels that would bring down the walls of Jericho (Joshua 5:14).

When Jezebel was threatening Elijah with death, he wanted

to give up. Then the angel of the Lord touched him and said, "Arise, eat!"

The prophet was fed and watered twice by the angel. That food gave him the strength of forty days and forty nights. (1 Kings 19:4-8).

Moses was in his daily routine tending the flock, when the angel of the Lord appeared to him in flames within a burning bush. When Moses saw that the bush was not burning up, he went over to investigate. It was the best thing he could have done! Imagine what Moses would have missed if he hadn't stepped aside for a moment from his day's normal routine.

It was an encounter with God that led him into his destiny and calling (Exodus 3).

We need to be aware of "unusual" happenings in our day-to-day routines, to be on our toes, living in expectancy of the supernatural. At any given moment during the day or night God may be trying to get our attention.

Let's be tuned in, like Moses was!

4. Angels come when we suffer for doing right

Daniel 6:22, 25-27: *"My God sent His angel and shut the lions' mouths and they have not harmed me, inasmuch as I was found innocent before Him; and also toward you, O king, I have committed no crime."*

... Then Darius the king wrote to all the peoples, nations and men of every language who were living in all the land: "May your peace abound! I make a decree that in all the dominion of my kingdom men are to fear and tremble before the God of Daniel; For He is the living God and enduring forever, And His kingdom is one which will not be destroyed, And His dominion will be forever. He delivers and rescues and performs signs and wonders In heaven and on earth, Who has also delivered Daniel from the power of the lions."

Doing the will of God can bring enemies. Daniel ended up in the lions' den. But God brought him out and he was vindicated!

When Jesus was on the cross, an angel came and strengthened Him (Luke 22:42-43).

1 Peter 1:12: *It was revealed to them that they were not serving themselves, but you, in these things which now have been announced to you through those who preached the gospel to you by the Holy Spirit sent from heaven – things into which angels long to look.* Angels cannot sing Amazing Grace! They don't know the Redemption Song, but they rejoice in heaven when one sinner repents (Luke 15:10).

The Angel Gabriel came to Mary and told her that God had decided to bless her in a wonderful way. Mary was confused and didn't understand what the angel meant when he explained that she was going to have a baby and she was to call Him Jesus.

In those days Mary would have been facing public humiliation in becoming pregnant without being married, and also not being able to defend herself. Her thoughts on it were to get married first, and then have a baby. Also according to the law she would have been put to death.

But God sent an angel to let her know that she was chosen for this by God, and was in the centre of His will. So she was not to be afraid. Mary told the angel she was willing to do whatever God wanted. Then the angel left her.

God sent an angel to encourage her, to reassure her and the vindicate her (Luke 1:34-38). And in Matthew 1:18-25 we read how an angel also came to Joseph in a dream, to tell him not to be afraid to take Mary as his wife. He had been planning to send her away secretly, because he was *"a righteous man."* But he obeyed the angel's instructions and took Mary as his wife. He was a good man and his heart pleased God.

5. Angels are not to be worshipped

Colossians 2:18: *Let no one keep defrauding you of your prize by delighting in self-abasement and the worship of the angels, taking his stand on visions he has seen, inflated without cause by his fleshly mind.*

There is only One who is worthy of our worship. Only One True God. Only One on the Throne and in control. He is the One who has the last word, who knows the end from the beginning.

God is the All Powerful One. There is no greater love than

His love. No greater power than His power. We were made with the need inside to worship someone or something – and if we don't worship God we will find someone or something else to worship!

Anything that we love and worship more than God is an idol. He is the only King – the King of kings and Lord of lords. He wants every part of our lives, to be living sacrifices on the altar for Him (Romans 12:1).

We were made to worship God, called to bring glory to Him, called to be fruitful for His Kingdom. We were made *by* God and made *for* God – to worship only Him.

There is only room for one king on the throne of our hearts – King Jesus.

6. Angels at the Second Coming

Matthew 24:31: *And He will send forth His angels with a great trumpet and they will gather together His elect from the four winds, from one end of the sky to the other.*

His glorious return! The angels will gather together the elect – what a day that will be! *But you have come to Mount Zion and to the city of the living God, the heavenly Jerusalem, and to myriads of angels* (Hebrews 12:22).

Angels were at the announcement of Jesus' birth (Luke 2:13-15).

In Revelation 7:1-3 we read that angels are on assignment. They are strong, and powerful and purposeful. We, as the Body of Christ, will judge and reward the angels (1 Corinthians 6:3).

Jesus will appear suddenly with His mighty angels, like a thief in the night. 2 Thessalonians 1:7-8: *...and to give relief to you who are afflicted and to us as well when the Lord Jesus will be revealed from heaven with His mighty angels in flaming fire, dealing out retribution to those who do not know God and to those who do not obey the gospel of our Lord Jesus.*

We need to make sure we are ready for His return, prepared to meet with Him who is our maker. We need to know Him as our Saviour, knowing that our sins are forgiven, and knowing that we are going to Heaven. We need to know that our lives are right with Him, and *then* we will welcome His return. It is so important to know that we will be taken up with Him, and not left behind on that great and wonderful day.

Mark 8:38: Jesus said, *"For whoever is ashamed of Me and My words in this adulterous and sinful generation, the Son of Man will also be ashamed of him when He comes in the glory of His Father with the holy angels."*

7. Everything is held together by God's Power

Colossians 1:15-17: *He is the image of the invisible God, the firstborn of all creation. For by Him all things were created, both in the heavens and on earth, visible and invisible, whether thrones or dominions or rulers or authorities—all things have been created through Him and for Him. He is before all things, and in Him all things hold together.*

No power is greater than His power. He rules and reigns over all. His Kingdom knows no end. He will make perfect all that concerns us. His Word is the greatest Authority – not man, not circumstances.

God fully accepts us and forgives us as we come to Him. He delights over us. As we confess our sins He will forgive us and cleanse us from all unrighteousness – every wrong thing we have ever done (1 John 1:8-9). But we need to forgive others as we are forgiven (Matthew 6:14).

This Mighty God of the Universe makes His home in us! The power of His Kingdom lives within us. As we say sorry for all the wrong things we have done, and ask Him into our heart, He comes! He transforms our lives by His Power at work within us. He makes us a brand-new person on the inside, with a new heart and new desires.

When one person gives their heart to Jesus, all the angels in Heaven rejoice! (Luke 15:10.) The miracle of new life in Jesus has happened in that person's heart, and it really is something to rejoice about!

Revelation 5:11-14: *Then I looked, and I heard the voice of many angels around the throne and the living creatures and the elders; and the number of them was myriads of myriads, and thousands of thousands, saying with a loud voice,*

"Worthy is the Lamb that was slain to receive power and riches and wisdom and might and honor and glory and blessing."

And every created thing which is in heaven and on the earth and under the earth and on the sea, and all things in them, I heard saying, "To Him who sits on the throne, and to the Lamb, be blessing and honor and glory and dominion forever and ever."

And the four living creatures kept saying, "Amen." And the elders fell down and worshiped.

Revelation 7:11-12: *And all the angels were standing around the throne and around the elders and the four living creatures; and they fell on their faces before the throne and worshiped God, saying, "Amen, blessing and glory and wisdom and thanksgiving and honor and power and might, be to our God forever and ever. Amen."*

Prayers

A prayer if you are already born again and would like to use it

Dear Lord Jesus, help me to know that I am always protected by You, strengthened by You, upheld by You and surrounded by Your angels and Your great unchanging love. You are my Helper and my Rescuer, and my Provider. You send Your angels to help me in troubled times and challenging times.

Help me to worship You and You alone, and not to love and worship anything more than You – to put You first in every part of my life.

In Jesus' Name. Amen.

A prayer if you would like to ask Jesus into your life

Lord Jesus, I thank You for dying from me on the cross. I am sorry for all the wrong things I have done in my life. Thank You that when I say sorry from my heart, You forgive me and wipe my slate completely clean. Please come into my life and fill me with Your Holy Spirit. Make me a brand-new person on the inside.

Thank You, Jesus. Amen.

If you prayed this second prayer, it's good to let someone know what you've just done. Also find a good church to go to, one that teaches about the Christian life, Jesus and the Bible, so you can be around other believers who can encourage you and help you.

23. Seven Truths about Being Sent with Vision

From this Chapter

We need to spend time, quality time, in God's presence in intimacy, hearing His voice and obeying Him. Many things happen in His presence: more than anywhere else.

If our vision is of God, it will burn in us like a fire, and through prayer it will get stronger over time. Our vision motivates us into action!

If we don't have a vision, we must ask God for one. Then God will birth one within us. And we will know it's from God, and it will bring excitement. Then we must add action to our vision – or it won't go anywhere!

Romans 10:15: *But how are they to preach unless they are sent? Just as it is written: "How beautiful are the feet of those who bring good news of good things!"*

1. Here am I. Send me

Isaiah 6:1-8: *In the year of King Uzziah's death I saw the Lord sitting on a throne, lofty and exalted, with the train of His robe filling the temple. Seraphim were standing above Him, each having six wings: with two each covered his face, and with two each covered his feet, and with two each flew. And one called out to another and said,*

"Holy, Holy, Holy, is the Lord of armies. The whole earth is full of His glory."

And the foundations of the thresholds trembled at the voice of him who called out, while the temple was filling with smoke. Then I said,

"Woe to me, for I am ruined! Because I am a man of unclean lips, And I live among a people of unclean lips; For my eyes have seen the King, the Lord of armies."

Then one of the seraphim flew to me with a burning coal in his hand, which he had taken from the altar with tongs. He touched my mouth with it and said, "Behold, this has touched your lips; and your guilt is taken away and atonement is made for your sin."

Then I heard the voice of the Lord, saying, "Whom shall I send, and who will go for Us?" Then I said, "Here am I. Send me!"

This happened in the temple after King Uzziah died. Uzziah was a good king, but at the height of his success he became very proud. He went beyond his authority by burning incense, which was something only the priests were allowed to do. Because he was raging at the priests, he was banned from the temple and became a leper for the rest of his life.

The death of King Uzziah caused Isaiah to see the King of kings! He saw Him in a vision *high and lifted up* (Isaiah 57:15-19). Isaiah surrendered his life, and he was cleansed and commissioned. The vision changed his whole life and ministry forever. "*Here am I. Send me*," he said.

We were in a meeting listening to an international evangelist sharing the Word of God, and his experience and some testimony. He told of an incident about a lady who had just lost her whole family in Ukraine.

He wanted to pray for her, but the language barrier was making it difficult. Then God stepped in, and as their eyes locked, he placed his hand on her shoulder and prayed for her.

She sobbed and sobbed for a long time. Then, when she looked up, her face was radiant. God had healed her broken heart. An amazing miracle! The Evangelist said that as he was praying for her, he heard these words in his head: "So send I you."

I was making notes at the time, but the next day God brought it back to me very strongly – just that phrase. He started talking to me about it and giving me a fresh revelation about what He had put within me – the Power and Authority of the Kingdom.

I did a lot of crying as the Holy Spirit was speaking to me and touching my heart and my spirit. Right then, I knew that I would never lay hands on someone again without remembering the words, "So send I You," and recognising more than ever before the power and authority God has put *within me* for signs, wonders and miracles. Thank God for our testimonies, and His Power at work within us.

John 20:21: *So Jesus said to them again, "Peace be to you; just as the Father has sent Me, I also send you."*

2. We are all sent

Luke 9:2: *And He sent them out to proclaim the kingdom of God and to perform healing.*

To be sent doesn't always mean we are leaving the country! Sometimes it does, but not always. We are all "sent", and the living resurrection power of Jesus Christ flows through us to a lost and dying world. It's good to know what our vision is – and who we are sent to, and where our place of influence is. Our gifts and our talents are a guide to our destiny and our vision

1 Timothy 4:14: *Do not neglect the spiritual gift within you,*

which was granted to you through words of prophecy with the laying on of hands by the council of elders.

Not neglecting the spiritual gift that is in us takes discipline – which reaps benefits. Progress and growth and moving on with God needs discipline. It's not an "in the mood" feeling. It's disciplining *ourselves*.

As we communicate with God regularly, and come into alignment with Him and His heart, the Holy Spirit draws from us who we are, and what we are called to do. This causes us to realise what we have been called to, and the vision that God has given us.

This is why we need to spend time, quality time, in God's presence in intimacy, hearing His voice and obeying Him. Many things happen in His presence: more than anywhere else. If our vision is of God, it will burn in us like a fire, and through prayer it will get stronger over time. Our vision motivates us into action!

Abraham was told to leave everything when he was seventy-five years old. He was an extremely rich man. If we are willing to let go, then God can trust us with more.

John 17:4: Jesus said, *"I glorified You on the earth by accomplishing the work which You have given Me to do."*

3. What vision is

Acts 26:19: *"For that reason, King Agrippa, I did not prove disobedient to the heavenly vision."*

Paul was not disobedient to the heavenly vision on the road to Damascus. Vision comes from God. It is seeing beyond where we are right now, and seeing it come to pass. We need to speak life into vision with the Word of God and with faith. It is activating our faith in the present, for what we see coming to pass in the future. Vision lights the pathway ahead. It's a strong, powerful, knowing where we are going. It takes hold of our hearts and our spirits.

Vision comes from the heart of God, and it is who He has made us to be, the very core of who we are. Every vision is unique, because we are all unique.

Vision takes us out of our comfort zone. There is always timing attached to the fulfilment of our vision – God's timing. It's good to write our vision down. Jesus knew His purpose, and focused on it all the time. We need to know that what we *are* doing is what we *ought* to be doing.

4. Setbacks and problems on the way

Habakkuk 2:3: *For the vision is yet for the appointed time; It hurries toward the goal and it will not fail. Though it delays, wait for it; For it will certainly come, it will not delay long.* There will always be things to deal with on our way to its fulfilment, but they cannot stop our vision without our permission!

The vision from God ought to be too big for us, beyond our capabilities. Alfred D Souza wrote, *"For a long time it seemed to me that life was about to begin – real life. But there was always some obstacle in the way, something to get through first, some unfinished business, time is still to be served, a debt to be paid. Then life would begin. At last it dawned on me that these obstacles were my life."*

When we come up against obstacles we become aware of things about ourselves we never knew. We find out how strong our faith is in God, and in ourselves. Obstacles are things to strengthen our faith, not to let go of our vision. We will regret the things that we didn't do, more than the things that we did. So when our vision looks too big for us – trust God, because nothing is too big for Him!

Mark 10:27: *Looking at them, Jesus said, "With people it is impossible, but not with God; for all things are possible with God."*

5. We need a vision to be "Sent"

Proverbs 29:18: *Where there is no vision, the people are unrestrained, But happy is one who keeps the Law.*

If we don't have a vision, we must ask God for one. Then God will birth one within us. And we will know it's from God, and it will bring excitement. Then we must add action to our vision – or it won't go anywhere!

Don't believe the lies that say anything from God is easy and straightforward. There are things to overcome, but God will get us there if we are walking in His way.

It's great when we start to see fruit from our vision. The Holy Spirit is always breathing freshness on us as we seek God. Let's always be ready to cooperate with Him.

Speak the life and the truth of the Word of God into it. Keep it fresh and sharp, and stay focused. Declare a fresh touch and breath of God on it. Don't lose sight of its fulfilment. Don't let obstacles stop you.

Press in and press on in God's strength. Don't give the enemy any footholds. We need to keep praying for a fresh awareness and revelation of our vision.

Romans 10:15: *But how are they to preach unless they are sent? Just as it is written: "How beautiful are the feet of those who bring good news of good things!"*

6. We are equipped with all that we need

1 Kings 18:46: *Then the hand of the Lord was on Elijah, and he belted his cloak around his waist and outran Ahab to Jezreel.*

We have everything that we need to do all that God has called us to do. Whatever we face is not beyond the Power and Authority and the Hand of God. We need to recognise His Power at work within us, and see increase of that. God has made us to be more than conquerors! We are being awakened and stirred by God in these days. Nothing will stop His plan and purpose.

How hungry are we for more of God? Are we pursuing Him and more of His presence in our lives? Let's raise the level of our expectation, and stretch beyond our own restricted limitations. We need the fresh breath of the Holy Spirit more and more.

Ephesians 3:20: *Now to Him who is able to do far more abundantly beyond all that we ask or think, according to the power that works within us.*

Ask bigger – to reach our full potential in God – to be everything He requires of us in every way – to be more and more like Jesus!

7. Ten points to finish

* We are all sent.
* Where are you sent, and who to?
* What burns like a fire within you?
* What are you willing to walk away from?
* Are you doing what you ought to be doing?
* Are you moving out of your comfort zone?
* Vision comes from a burning desire within.
* We must raise the level of our expectation.
* How hungry are we for more of God?
* Wherever we are, God meets us there.

A prayer for vision – if you would like to use it

Dear Lord Jesus, please give me a fresh revelation of who I am in You, and Your Power and Authority that is within me. Help me to be willing to do anything You want me to do, to fulfil my destiny.

If I don't have a vision, please birth one in me – and help me to fulfil it.

I ask it in Jesus' Name. Amen

For more detail
please contact Lin Wills:
hello@lenandlin.com

I live in England, and my husband Len and I are part of Intercessors for Bristol. We long to see God move in revival, and have an itinerant ministry which covers a circuit of churches in our city and beyond on a regular basis.

We love to meet with God's people and encourage one another in His presence through worship, the Word of God, and the gifts of the Holy Spirit.

Our vision is to see God's people rise up in victory, and set on fire to be the powerful army God called us to be. We want to see all that the enemy has stolen from God's people restored back to the Church, and prayer and intercession released like never before.

Website:
www.lenandlin.com

eBook editions of all individual chapters are published by White Tree Publishing, available from most eBook distributors

Volume 1 contains the first sixty-three titles in the 7 Series.

eBook ISBN: 978-1-913950-73-6
Paperback ISBN: 978-1-913950-72-9

About White Tree Publishing

White Tree Publishing publishes mainstream evangelical Christian literature for people of all ages, with 250 titles available. We aim to make our eBooks available free for all eBook devices, but some distributors will only list our books free at their discretion, and may make a small charge for some titles – but they are still great value! All our books are fully typeset. No "photocopies" or bad OCR! Long sentences and paragraphs are broken into shorter lengths, and modern punctuation is used for easier reading. Many books are sensitively abridged.

WHITE TREE PUBLISHING

wtpbristol@gmail.com

https://whitetreepublishing.com/

Printed in Great Britain
by Amazon

45109121R00106